FENG SHUI

DOS & TABOOS

Also by Angi Ma Wong

Feng Shui Dos & Taboos
Feng Shui Dos & Taboos for Financial Success
Feng Shui Dos & Taboos for Love

❊❊❊

Hay House Titles of Related Interest

Feng Shui for the Soul, by Denise Linn
Help Me to Heal, by Bernie S. Siegel, M.D., and Yosaif August
Home Design with Feng Shui A–Z, by Terah Kathryn Collins
The Power of the Mind to Heal, by Joan Z. Borysenko, Ph.D.
Space Clearing A–Z, by Denise Linn
The Western Guide to Feng Shui, by Terah Kathryn Collins
The Western Guide to Feng Shui for Romance,
by Terah Kathryn Collins
The Western Guide to Feng Shui: Room by Room,
by Terah Kathryn Collins
You Can Heal Your Life, by Louise L. Hay

❊❊❊

FENG SHUI

DOs & TABOOs

HAY HOUSE, INC.
Carlsbad, California
London • Sydney • Johannesburg
Vancouver • Hong Kong • New Delhi

Published and distributed in the United States by: Hay House, Inc.: www.hayhouse.com • ***Published and distributed in Australia by:*** Hay House Australia Pty. Ltd.: www.hayhouse.com.au • ***Published and distributed in the United Kingdom by:*** Hay House UK, Ltd.: www.hayhouse.co.uk • ***Published and distributed in the Republic of South Africa by:*** Hay House SA (Pty), Ltd.: orders@psdprom.co.za • ***Distributed in Canada by:*** Raincoast: www.raincoast.com • ***Published in India by:*** Hay House Publishers India: www.hayhouseindia.co.in

Editorial supervision: Jill Kramer *Design:* Amy Gingery

Library of Congress Control No. 2004103357

ISBN 13: 978-1-4019-0334-3
ISBN 10: 1-4019-0334-7

09 08 07 06 5 4 3 2
1st printing, January 2005
2nd printing, November 2006

Printed in Canada by Transcontinental

CONTENTS

A PERSONAL MESSAGE

The theme of this book is how to achieve good health and peace of mind through feng shui in a world of constant change.

According to the Chinese calendar, we're currently celebrating the advent of the lunar year 4702 of the Wood Monkey. While each new year is considered one of birth, new hope, and renewal, the Year of the Monkey is also one of learning, self-development, and cultivation; of finding one's path;

and of imagination, creativity, invention, and innovation. That's because the monkey is known for being curious and mischievous—and even as he gets into everything, he's constantly discovering new things.

In feng shui time, we're also welcoming the commencement of Period 8, the second to last in a 9-period, 180-year cycle, with the first day of the solar new year having begun on February 4, 2004. This is a time to get back to the basics as the element and influence of earth returns to dominate. Good riddance to Period 7 and its inherent violence and destruction, both natural and human-made, which have impacted these last few years since the millennium. We'll certainly never forget the shared traumas of September 11; the loss of the space shuttle *Columbia;* the wars, earthquakes, storms, and floods that have ravaged the globe; as well as the SARS epidemic—all of which touched and changed lives around the world.

In feng shui, it's important to pay attention to the omens and signs around us and listen to the messages that they're imparting, particularly in nature. I often wonder if I was the only one who noticed that it was on the first day of the Chinese Year of the Ram that most of *Columbia's* debris fell in the home state of

President Bush . . . just as he was deciding to declare war on terrorism and invade Iraq. If that tragedy wasn't a sign—literally and figuratively—from heaven, I don't know what would be.

❄❄❄

September 11, 2001, will forever remain etched in our consciousness. I liken that day to a shared, worldwide psychic earthquake that shattered our spirits, decimated our serenity and complacency, and left us all feeling vulnerable and unprotected—much like other defining moments have over time, including the day the stock market crashed in 1929, Franklin Roosevelt's death, the Pearl Harbor attack, the atomic bombs dropping in Japan, and John F. Kennedy's assassination. Each of these historical moments represented a shock to our peace of mind, a trauma shared by many, as well as a feeling of loss of control of our lives.

After September 11, we immediately drew those around us together—we shared our individual experiences, which in turn helped us feel better, knowing that others had gone through the same awful thing. As the president of my Rotary Club, I seriously considered cancelling our meeting that was scheduled for that evening. Yet I didn't want to be alone that night; instead, I wanted to surround myself with friends whom I knew, respected, and loved. During my welcoming remarks, I shared how and why I'd come to my decision. Afterward, a visiting Rotarian who happened to be a psychologist stood up and validated my actions as the best thing I could have done for everyone present.

Through our faith, and through each other, we can draw comfort and peace in times of sorrow, and we should allow ourselves to share our thoughts and feelings, thus diluting the intensity of our loss. Eventually, after acceptance, there will come a time when we'll naturally feel that

it's time to move on, and that's when we'll need to focus on our priorities. And that's where feng shui comes in.

We become personally empowered when we take action and are in charge of the details of our lives and our surroundings, even when (or as) things may feel as if they're falling apart around us. While we can't control the weather, the economy, or other people, we and only we are in charge of our thoughts, words, and deeds. And at the very least, we can control what's in our own spaces, in our homes, and in our workplaces. Feng shui helps us do just that; therefore, we become empowered.

Just remember that we reap what we sow. So if we plant pumpkin seeds, we'll get pumpkins; if we plant acorns, we'll get oak trees; and if we "sow the seeds of love" (which was the Rotary International theme two years ago) and send out positive thoughts, we'll reap the benefits and harvest of those seeds a thousandfold in unexpected or surprising ways. The opposite is true, too: If we scatter thoughts, words, and deeds of negativity, their harvest will return in many forms to haunt, undermine, or destroy us. This is a basic truth in nature, in life, and in feng shui.

One of the greatest gifts we have is our home planet. As stewards of Earth, it is our sacred and moral duty to take care of it, as well as each other. Feng shui is a philosophy that allows us to live a more natural, spiritual, and intuitive life while doing just that. It's not surprising that with the way we're polluting our water, soil, and air, Mother Earth has lashed back at us with a plethora of natural disasters. Yet if we take care of the planet, it will take care of us. We must honor, respect, and bless Earth's power and its gifts.

As you read this book, you'll see how the Chinese link the element of earth to our physical health and well-being. This is one of the fundamental beliefs I instill into my feng shui practice, teaching, and writing. I truly believe that the popularity of this subject has grown from the spiritual poverty that many people feel today, and that traditional religions have not been able to correct. The same holds true for modern medicine, science, and technology—too much left-brain thinking has dominated the past millennium, which is now being replaced by alternative philosophies of healing, thinking, creativity, intuition, and other right-brain functions. It's again a matter of balancing the yin and yang. It's imperative to our health and peace of mind to embrace and focus on what really is at the core of our being.

❊❊❊

Thanks to all of you who have shared your thoughts and experiences with me through your correspondence, telling your personal stories of how my work has changed your lives. Your word of mouth has made *Feng Shui Dos & Taboos* and its gift-book offspring *(Feng Shui Dos & Taboos for Love, Feng Shui Dos & Taboos for Financial Success)*, as well as my *Feng Shui Room-by-Room Home Design Kit, Feng Shui Desk for Success Tool Kit,* and *Feng Shui Garden Design Kit* into best-selling titles. (All of these are available through **www.FengShuiLady.com.)**

Your support, appreciation of my work, and encouragement enriches my life, giving it balance and meaning. Ultimately, that's what we all need to be healthy and to enjoy serenity: to be centered and well grounded. For inner peace and well-being, you need not go anywhere but within yourself. For good health, you need not look anywhere else but in your surroundings, which you've created. Feng shui is only one leg of a table—you need to balance the intellectual, physical, and spiritual legs, too, or your table of life will be unstable.

Please keep in mind that feng shui must be practiced with strong intentions and pure hearts. This wonderful ancient Chinese environmental system of placement (or "house fortune-telling," as I like to call it), is to be used to your personal advantage; but at the same time, it needs to be done prudently so that you don't bring injury or harm to another. You see, only *you* can reach into yourself to discover your soul's own light; only you can choose to use feng shui to create a healing, nurturing, and energizing home or workplace; only you can choose to balance your life.

I remain passionate about perpetuating the cultural integrity and excellence in my practice and consulting, writing, and lecturing about feng shui; and I'm honored to be your guide as you endeavor to reach your goals through this ancient system of environmental harmony. In fact, I have a dream that one day I'll see the following words on the walls of every school and place of worship, which are as true today as when they were written some 2,500 years ago:

If there is light in the soul
there will be beauty in the person.
If there is beauty in the person
there will be harmony in the house.
If there is harmony in the house
there will be order in the country.
If there is order in the country
there will be peace in the world.

— Chinese proverb

While the apple on each page reminds us that it's to keep the doctor away, in Chinese, the word for apple is *ping*, which is a homonym for *peace*. May you enjoy the blessings of both good health and peace in your heart, home, and world.

Best regards,
Angi Ma Wong

FengShuiLady®

Websites: **www.FengShuiLady.com**
www.AsianConnections.com

E-mail: **angi@FengShuiLady.com**

I'm personally familiar with the advice contained within this book. One night while bathing, I discovered a lump in one of my breasts. To make a long story short, the tumor was malignant and was removed, followed by chemotherapy and radiation.

As soon as I got home from the hospital following my surgery, I immediately changed the position of my bed, as I didn't want it to be in the same direction as it was in when I developed the cancer. It was during my subsequent recuperation and recovery that I decided that life was too short and precious to *not* pursue my dreams, two of which were to write a book and start my own business. H. Jackson Brown, Jr.'s words perfectly described my frame of mind at the time: "When you look back on your life, you'll regret the things you didn't do more than the ones you did."

Now looking back 15 years later, I see that my cancer experience was the catalyst for the wonderful discovery of my mission in life: to help others through the gifts that heaven has bestowed upon me. My faith and feng shui work have centered and grounded me, bringing so many blessings in the form of unique experiences, old and new friends, personal and professional growth, travel, and lots more. But without good health, none of it would matter.

"The emperor is rich, but he cannot buy one extra year."
— Chinese proverb

This saying is so true. The United States may be the richest nation in the world, yet its people are certainly not the healthiest. Nor are the wealthiest people in *any* country enjoying the best health, the most happiness, or the greatest sense of well-being. Rather, the opposite is true: Those who live the simplest lives, free from worry, stress, fast food, and even faster-paced lifestyles are healthiest and enjoy longer lives. Longevity is their reward for having balance and harmony in life, and freedom from the dramatic ups and downs that continually disrupt our tranquility. And having a support system is vitally important, which includes people and pets who give and return love and comfort.

Now, no book on feng shui and its relationship to good health would be complete without mention of how the mind and body are interrelated.

	MIND	
Kindness	HEART	Strength
	BODY	

Notice in this illustration that the mind and heart are on the same staff that holds up kindness and strength. Also note the close relationships between lifestyle and health: We *are* what we think, eat, and do to our mind, heart, and body. The two arms of strength and kindness are the hands that reach out to the world—if we aren't mindful of or don't take responsibility for our own good health, we won't be well enough or live long enough to enjoy the fruits of our labors. After all, some people are so busy making a living that they forget to live.

It's critical to understand how feng shui is a part of a holistic philosophy whose fundamentals are shared with traditional Chinese medicine (TCM). Once you've grasped these shared principles, you'll realize that they're like a two-cord braid: feng shui takes care of what surrounds us (our environment), while TCM takes care of what's within our body.

Feng Shui (and TCM) Basics

Human beings and other forms of life on Earth evolved to depend on two things for survival: fresh air and clean water. In Chinese, this translates to *feng* (wind) and *shui* (water). Feng shui shares the same three fundamental concepts that TCM does. In fact, acupressure, acupuncture, chi gong, martial arts, tai chi, traditional and folk practices, and the use of herbs and food cures all integrate with feng shui to make up a natural and intuitive way of living that can be practiced and enjoyed by everyone.

The **first** concept that feng shui shares with TCM is the flow of *chi*—the universal, cosmic energy that surrounds and connects us all. In nature, this energy travels in wavy or undulating currents, like those we see in the ripples of a flag moving with the breeze, or as rainwater meandering down from the mountains. Traveling at a moderate speed, this type of feng and shui are considered beneficial, as breezes cool and clean the air, and slow-moving rivers deposit rich silt on their inside curves and deltas.

Conversely, nature doesn't tend to provide perfectly straight lines (except in short segments such as in sugar or bamboo canes). When wind or water is at its most violent and destructive, it usually travels in a straight fashion, which we see in a rushing river right before it thunders over a cliff to create a waterfall, or in stormy winds that blow so hard that they bend the branches and trunks of trees. When we see images of a flood destroying and sweeping away everything in its path, the water is generally moving in a straight line, following the human-made streets of a town. Therefore, such energy is called *sha chi,* or "killing energy."

In people, chi moves in hundreds of channels called *meridians,* and when there's an obstruction or blockage of this beneficial energy in the human body, then disease, illness, and other maladies occur. Consequently, the practices of acupuncture, acupressure, and moxibustion—as well as the use of herbs, diet, nutrition, exercise, and so on—were developed to keep a person's vital chi flowing for good mental, emotional, and physical health.

The **second** concept of feng shui is that of harmony and balance. To the Chinese, this is represented by the *tai chi* symbol, featuring the teardrop-shaped halves known as *yin* and *yang*—yin, meaning "dark," is the feminine half: soft, negative, passive, and nurturing; yang means "light," and it's the masculine half: hard, positive, and aggressive. Yet yin and yang are *not* opposites of each other; rather, they're halves of a whole. And keep in mind that the S demarcation is never fixed—for example, when you're happy, healthy, and upbeat, you're enjoying positive yang energy, and the light side is greater in size; however, when you're tired, depressed, ill, angry, sad, or experiencing other physical, emotional, or psychological distress, the yin energy dominates, and the darker side becomes larger.

Figure A –
The Tai Chi Symbol

In TCM, our bodies require balance, too, so the Chinese characterize all foods as being either yin or yang. Basically, yin foods are fruits and vegetables, while yang foods are meats and proteins. Meat and dairy products are considered "dirty," while plants are considered "clean." In addition, wearing natural fibers such as cotton, linen, and silk is considered to be healthy, compared to adorning our bodies with toxic, artificially made fibers containing chemicals that are then absorbed into our bodies through the skin, our largest organ. When you consider the preponderance of synthetics in our homes and workplaces, it's no wonder that the high incidence of cancer is linked to our environments.

The **third** major idea in both feng shui and TCM is that of the five elements: wood, fire, earth, metal, and water. These interact with each other in two different ways, generative and destructive. In the generative relationship, one element is the source for the next; while in the destructive cycle, an element can destroy another. These relationships aren't necessarily positive or negative, and we can see them at work in nature.

When we're sick or troubled, it's believed that there's a blockage or obstruction in the body's chi flow, an imbalance of yin or yang, or a clash of the elements. An old Chinese proverb reminds us: *Ills come into and out of the body by the way of the mouth.* In short, we are what we eat and say.

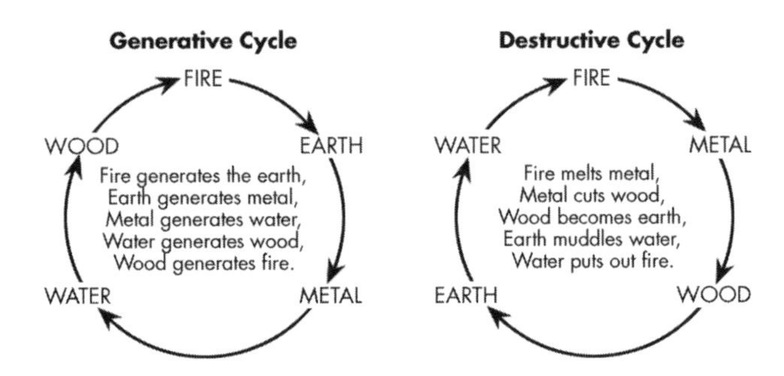

Figure B – The Generative and Destructive Element Cycles

The Five-Element Feng Shui Health Chart

While Western medicine focuses on treating the symptoms of a disease or illness, thus pushing its root cause deeper into the body, the Chinese focus on curing the whole person from the inside out, targeting his or her spirit, mind, and body. Although Western medicine has only recently made the mind-body connection to healing, the Chinese have subscribed to it for more than 4,000 years. Today we have enough research to support what the Chinese know: that diet and nutrition affect our mental, emotional, and physical health. We also know that a positive, cheerful yang attitude can help to heal the yin effects of disease and illness. Banish negative thoughts and emotions from your life, and don't be surprised when many of your physical ailments disappear.

If you have trouble remembering whether to feed a cold and starve a fever (or vice versa), just flush out the impurities in your body by starving both! It's the Chinese way to support the body's efforts to heal itself by going on a light or all-liquid diet, so the body isn't overworked by having to digest heavier foods. But remember that prevention is almost always easier and cheaper than any cure: Your good health and peace of mind come from your choices in diet, exercise, nutrition, and moderation.

This handy chart should help break all this down for you:

The Five-Element Feng Shui Health Chart

Element	WOOD	FIRE	EARTH	METAL	WATER
Direction	E, SE	S	SW, NE	W, NW	N
Season	Spring	Summer		Autumn	Winter
Organs	Liver, gall bladder	Heart, small intestine	Stomach, spleen, pancreas	Lungs, large intestines	Bladder, kidneys
Body part	Hips	Eyes	Hands	Head	Ears
Flavor	Sour	Bitter	Sweet	Hot	Salty
Sense	Sight	Taste	Touch	Smell	Hearing
Emotion	Anger	Joy	Nostalgia	Sadness	Fear
Voice	Shouting	Laughter	Singing	Crying	Groaning
Action	Twitching	Itching	Hiccuping	Coughing	Shivering
Climate	Wind	Heat	Humidity	Dryness	Cold

The Five Components of Destiny

The Chinese believe that feng shui is only one of the five components that make up our destinies. The other four are fate, luck, charity, and education.

Fate represents all the circumstances of our birth, which include time, family, ethnicity, status, socioeconomic conditions, and so forth. Luck consists of three different kinds: heaven, human-made, and pure. The company president who took his son to kindergarten on the first day of school had good heaven luck . . . his hundreds of employees who perished that same morning at the World Trade Center did not. Human-made luck is taking part in creating your own opportunities in order to bring you good fortune.

As an aside, I love telling about my own personal experience involving pure luck. In 1989 I came away from that cancer experience with a decision to start my own business, and in the course of things, I called the phone company to order a number. The representative offered six numbers from her computer for me to choose from, and my selection was an easy-to-remember sequential number.

The next day, a technician showed up at the door to install the new phone. Even though

I'd written my new number down, I asked him what it was anyway.

"8818," he replied.

"Would you repeat that again?" I gasped.

"8818."

"That's not the number I chose."

"Well, it's yours now."

"Do you know how lucky that number is?"

You see, in Chinese, 8818 sounds like "prosperity, prosperity, guaranteed prosperity." In less than 24 hours, my original choice had been installed on someone else's phone, and by pure luck that very auspicious number—8818—became my business line (which it is to this day).

Now my Chinese-speaking friends who see my phone number invariably ask me who I know at the phone company!

The next component that makes up our destiny is charity: our doing good deeds and sending out positive energy into the universe, or reaping what we sow (karma). Last, but not least, is self-cultivation and education—we should always be developing personally, professionally, physically, mentally, spiritually, and emotionally. Keep the following quotations in mind:

"Shoot for the moon. Even if you miss it,
you'll land among the stars."
— Les Brown

"Imagination is more important than knowledge."
— Albert Einstein

Schools of Feng Shui

It's been said that there have been more than 30 schools or forms of feng shui over time. But two schools have emerged as the most popular in the world: the traditional, classical Compass School and the Black Sect Tantric Tibetan Buddhist School. Both transpose the octagon called the *bagua* on various rooms to determine what to place where within a space, and both assign different aspects of one's life to the various areas of a room—but they do these things in dramatically different fashions.

Even though I'm a classically trained, traditional Compass School practitioner, I've been practicing, writing, and teaching an integrated form of feng shui for many years—and I'm happy to share that information with you here.

The Compass School

In the Compass School, which is more than 3,000 years old and is practiced all over the world, a compass (Chinese or Western) is used to identify a space's magnetic North first, after which the remaining seven directions fit into place. The compass directions are fixed and constant; that is, North is always North in a room, office, or garden; South is always South, and so forth. The bagua map subsequently matches the eight zones formed by a grid placed over a space; and all eight areas are associated with different aspects of one's life, as well as the eight cardinal and secondary compass directions of N, NE, E, SE, S, SW, W, and NW.

The following list explains the eight compass directions and what they represent in the Compass School:

- **North (N):** Career and business success; black; winter; water; metal element; tortoise; the number 1

- **Northeast (NE):** Love of learning; spiritual, intellectual, mental, and emotional growth; turquoise, blue, or green; winter becoming spring; fire; earth element; the number 8

- **East (E):** Family, harmony, health, and prosperity; new beginnings; green, black, or blue; spring; wood element; water; dragon; the number 3

- **Southeast (SE):** Wealth, prosperity, and abundance; green or purple; spring becoming summer; wood element; water; the number 4

- **South (S):** Fame and fortune; longevity; festivity and joy; red; summer; wood element; fire; bird; the number 9

- **Southwest (SW):** Love, marriage, romance, relationships, and spouses; teamwork; gold, yellow, red, pink, or white; summer becoming autumn; earth element; fire; the number 2

- **West (W):** Children; creativity; white or silver; autumn; metal element; earth; tiger; the number 7

- **Northwest:** Father; helpful people, mentors, and benefactors; interests outside the home; trade; travel; gray, white, or yellow; autumn becoming winter; metal element; earth; the number 6

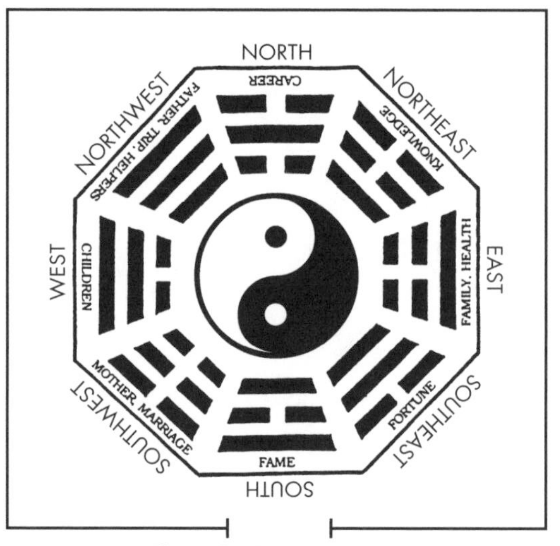

Figure C – The Bagua Map

Dir.	Color	Animal	No.	Element	Season
N	Black, blue	Tortoise	1	Water	Winter
NE	Turquoise		8	Earth	Winter to Spring
E	Green, blue	Dragon	3	Wood	Spring
SE	Green, purple		4	Wood	Spring to Summer
S	Red, purple	Phoenix	9	Fire	Summer
SW	Yellow, pink, red		2	Earth	Summer to Fall
W	White, metallic	Tiger	7	Metal	Fall
NW	Gray, metallic		6	Metal	Fall to Winter

Figure D – Compass School Directions

The Black Sect School

The Black Sect Tantric Tibetan Buddhist School of feng shui has been popularized in the United States in the last two decades, although its roots trace back to Buddhism. This practice doesn't need or use a compass at all. As in the Compass School, the bagua octagon governs certain aspects of one's life, but these are called "aspirations" (or goals). What distinguishes this form of feng shui from others is that the bagua rotates, room by room, depending on where the main entrance is. For instance, the center of the wall where the main entrance is located is always the Career area.

The Black Sect School also relies greatly on its "Nine Cures": wind chimes and bells; crystals; mirrors; lights; plants and flowers; aquariums and fishbowls; moving or powered objects; heavy objects; and bamboo flutes.

The list below describes what each area of a room represents according to the Black Sect School:

- **Front Center** (at the entrance looking into the room): Career; black or white; fountains; water

- **Left Front:** Knowledge, self-development, and success; personal goals and health; blue, black, or green; books

- **Left Center:** Family and ancestors; health; blue or green; heirlooms; shrines; photos

- **Left Rear:** Wealth, prosperity, abundance, and material things of value; red, purple, blue, or green; fountains, aquariums, and fish; banners

- **Center Rear** (across from main entrance): Fame and fortune; red or green; candles and fireplaces; awards and diplomas

- **Right Rear:** Marriage, relationships, spouse, and romance; mother; yellow

- **Right Center:** Children and creativity; white; metal; arts and crafts, toys, and games

- **Right Front:** Friends and supportive and helpful people; travel; father; black, white, or gray; religious icons

Take a moment to look at how different two adjoined rooms look from the perspectives of the Compass and Black Sect Schools as shown in the identical floor plans below. You've probably figured out that you can't mix these two forms of feng shui because where you place your enhancements will differ significantly from the Compass School to the Black Sect School.

Now take a few minutes to compare and understand the differences between these two popular forms of feng shui, and then choose the one that feels right for you. Whichever it is, please be consistent and use common sense.

SE S SW SE S SW

E *Kitchen* W E *Dining Room* W

NE N NW NE N NW

Figure E – The Compass School Map

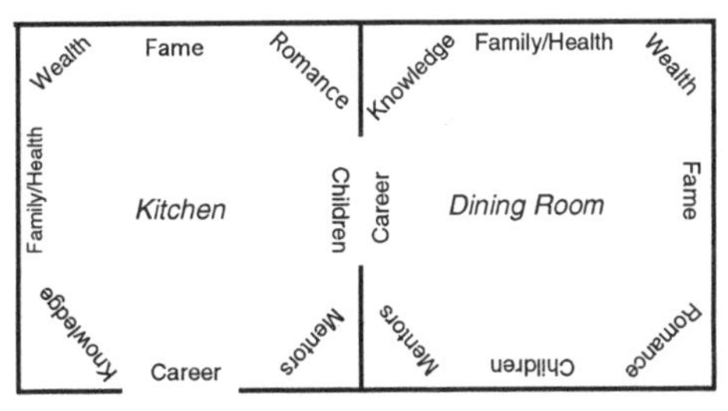

Figure F – The Black Sect School Map

Using Feng Shui to Maintain Your Health and Well-being

When you practice feng shui properly, you'll first notice the difference in your environment—your body, mind, spirit, and energy level. Good feng shui makes you feel wonderful because you've aligned your personal energy with your home or office. You may sleep better and even require less rest, yet wake up refreshed and raring to go. You may become more energized, achieve greater success at work, get along better with your family members and colleagues, and find yourself being more productive and ultimately more prosperous.

To get started, notice that each one of the eight compass directions is associated with different things, including aspects of one's life, colors, numbers, seasons, symbols, elements, parts and organs of the body, animals, and shapes. Also keep in mind my acronym *CANE*, which will help you put the right (C)olor, (A)nimal symbol, (N)umber, and (E)lement in the right place.

In addition, when I arrive at any location, four major things concern me. The **land formation** is the first. For both the living and the dead, a mountain or hill behind a residence or grave provides protection. Graves are often carved into hills and resemble a horseshoe to permit a good flow of cosmic chi energy; likewise, this same configuration is desired in the homes of the living. A horseshoe or armchair shape allows the two ends to capture entering energy, just as the arms of a chair keep your energy in the seat while you're sitting.

It's also auspicious if the site's location is halfway up a hill with a wide view in front, preferably of water. Water represents wealth, development, and prosperity, and the sight of it is especially auspicious. This is why you'll find an aquarium or fish tank near the entrances of most

Asian restaurants—the pumping water replicates the waves and flow found in lakes, rivers, and oceans, which brings prosperity. The location of a home in relation to the roads leading to it is also a consideration. Because *sha chi* (or "killing energy") moves in straight lines, it shouldn't be directed toward any structures. This precludes good feng shui at lots that are located at the end of cul-de-sacs or at the intersection of two roads that form a T. The rule of thumb is that if your office, lot, or home is illuminated by the headlights of vehicles traveling on a road toward it, it is the target of *sha chi*.

The second major consideration is the **plants and animals** that are found naturally on the site. If the location supports life with fresh breezes and clean-running water, it already has an advantage. Throw thriving flora and flourishing fauna into the mix, and you've got good feng shui. I always use my five senses when assessing a property: Is the sun warming my face? Do I hear birds singing in the background? Are there little critters scurrying around in tall grasses or weeds? Does the earth beneath my feet smell good and fertile? What do the rocks, hills, and trees on the property look like? Are the plants thriving, or dead or dying?

Next, I consider the **historical and spiritual events** that have occurred on the property. If you're looking at pre-owned homes, ask your Realtor why the current residents are moving away. Bankruptcy, murder, divorce, suicide, and other unfortunate occurrences all emanate great dark yin energy and must be removed before you move in. (No matter how good the asking price is, would you *really* want to live in Nicole Brown Simpson's condo or the palatial home in which the Heaven's Gate followers committed mass suicide?)

It's also wise to take note of how smooth or bumpy your acquisition of the property is, and pay attention to any messages you may pick up along the way. If things go smoothly and in a timely fashion, consider that your plans are in line with heaven's intent. On the other hand, if you seem to be encountering many hurdles or obstacles on the way to acquiring your new home, condo, or office, it's worthwhile to reevaluate the situation. You may feel strongly or emotionally about insisting on going forth with your plans, but if things start going dramatically wrong in your life after you take ownership, you'll realize the price of opposing heaven's plan.

The fourth major consideration is that of **human-made structures in the vicinity** of the site. Whether you're living in a studio apartment or a $200 million mansion, feng shui is seriously affected by what surrounds you. Take a good, hard look around your property, and start observing what could affect you. For example, each of the following will exert an influence: roads, bridges, and tunnels; lampposts; churches, temples, or steeples; businesses (and their functions); office and other buildings; canals, drainage ditches, flood channels, and washes; radio, television, and other broadcast antennas and towers; cemeteries, mortuaries, crematories, mausoleums, and memorial parks; hospitals, clinics, and schools; parks and golf courses; oil derricks, sewers, manholes, and hydrants; transportation centers such as railroad and subway stations; and so on.

By now you should have a good idea of how holistic the practice of feng shui is and how it relates to your spiritual, emotional, mental, and physical health and well-being. While other books may tell you that the area of health is governed by the compass direction of East, you can see from the Five-Element Health Chart of Feng Shui on page 33 that you must focus your feng shui activities in *all* directions.

Don't make the mistake of concentrating your efforts in only one area, only to neglect another. Feng shui, just like everything in your mind and body, must work together as an integrated whole, much like the hundreds of parts of an automobile or airplane, or even something as simple as a string of holiday lights. All components must work in concert with each other—so be mindful of the details of your diet as well as those that affect the *quality* of your life. There's not much point in living a long life if your later years are spent bedridden, in squalor, poverty, loneliness, and depression.

Don't overlook the details! Remember that Goliath was killed by a single stone from a slingshot; the *Titanic* was speeding when it hit the iceberg; *Challenger* was brought down by the failure of a simple, low-tech O-ring seal; and the *Columbia* tragedy was caused by a few loose tiles. Similarly, choosing to stay up late tonight may contribute to drowsiness that could cause you to rear-end another vehicle tomorrow.

Start your changes now, and keep a journal of what you do, day by day, and then record the results. But be patient—nothing unique or wonderful was created instantly.

In conclusion, remember the "3 Golden Rules of the Feng Shui Lady":

1. If it isn't broken, don't fix it. Ask yourself if you're happy, healthy, and prosperous: If the answers are yes, yes, and yes, then only fine-tune or make minor changes in your life. You don't want to make major overhauls and upset the blessings and good things you already have.

2. If you don't see it, it isn't there. Feng shui is a mental, practical, metaphysical, and spiritual process that uses a range of strategies—

including assessment, addition, camouflage, removal, deflection, transformation, and protection.

3. Everything is fixable. Feng shui offers hope, empowerment, and a marvelous opportunity for taking charge and being proactive in order to change your life.

Using your own personal taste, budget, creativity, and intentions, you can create a nurturing, rejuvenating home or workplace that supports your dreams and goals. A new life awaits you today through the wonder of feng shui—so get your compass ready, and embark on your path to great health and well-being right now!

FENG SHUI

DOS & TABOOS

Do locate your family, memorial, or religious altar in a quiet, respectful location that's away from the flow of traffic in your home.

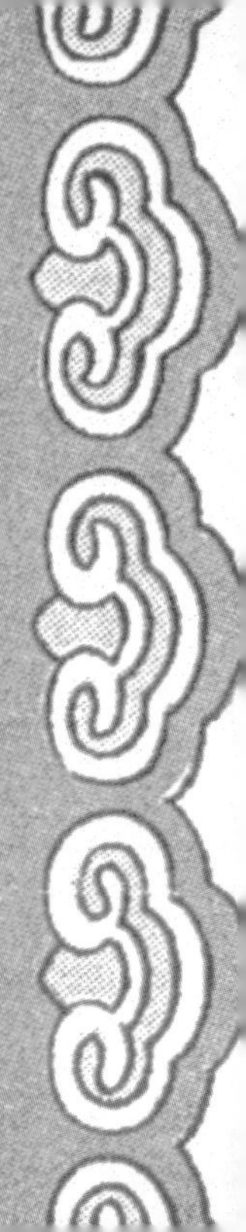

Don't erect an altar outdoors unless it's raised off the soil on bricks, stones, or a plat-form.

Do cover your out-door altar to protect it from the elements.

Don't put your altar in an area that's near, next to, under, or across from stairs or a bathroom.

Do position the altar in your business up on a high location that's facing the main entrance.

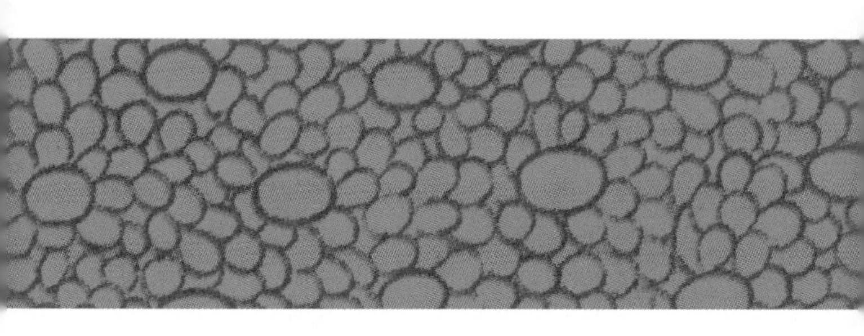

Don't place your family altar in a busy or noisy area of your home or place of business. Constant activity disturbs the energy near it, which is considered very disrespectful of the deity or family member the altar honors.

Do face an altar toward the main entrance to your home to provide protection and comfort to all who enter.

Do place a dog statue near your front door for protection.

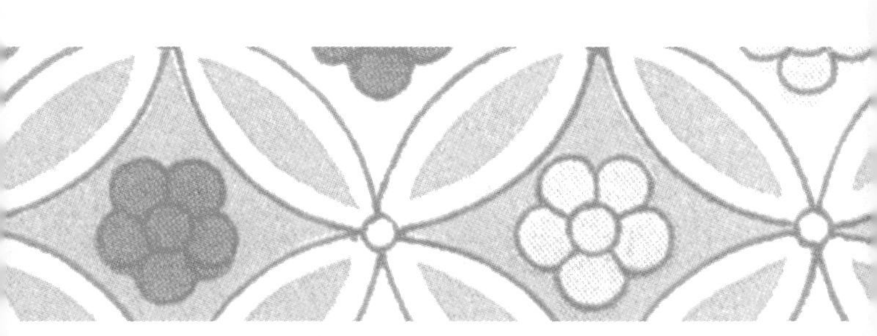

Do put a crystal or black-colored turtle, which is a symbol of protection and business prosperity, in the N.

Do place the Chinese unicorn (called the *chi ling,* or *kirin* in Japanese) in your home, as it represents long life as well as protection.

Do decorate with calm tigers, which symbolize children.

Do keep a gold-colored or metal tiger figurine in the W part of your bedroom to enhance your children energy, as white tigers represent the female and her children.

Do welcome a stray dog to your home, as it is considered an auspicious omen of good fortune coming to you (the Chinese character for *dog* and the lucky number *nine* are homonyms).

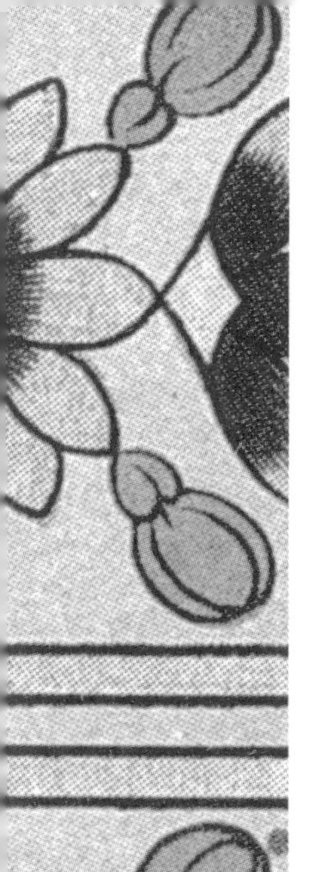

Do flank the front entrance of your home or business with a pair of protective Chinese fu dogs facing out.

Do put a wooden elephant in the E or SE, since elephants represent a family with many children.

Do try to discover the history of an antique before you purchase it for your home. Many relics from around the world are associated with yin activities such as death, healing, and ceremonial purposes.

Do be sure to have a proper balance of male and female images in the art-work you display in your home.

Don't bring items and artifacts associated with death, violence, or destruction into your home or office. These include souvenirs from the *Titanic,* the World Trade Center, or the Pyramids; and used swords or other weapons.

Do accessorize your home so that it's gender-neutral, allowing all guests to feel welcome.

Do decorate your home and office with uplifting art and images that inspire or calm you during your day.

Do keep your walls balanced with an equal amount of covered and uncovered space.

Do balance the active, bright, straight, and hard properties of yang with the passive, dark, curvy, and soft attributes of yin throughout your workplace, home, and garden.

Do keep a balance of quiet and active things to do during the day. Remember, you must experience valleys to appreciate life's peaks, and there must be rain before there can be rainbows.

"If you hurry through long days,
you will hurry through short years."
— Chinese proverb

Don't ever place rice, the traditional Chinese symbol of abundance, wealth, and fertility, any- where near a bath- room or toilet.

Do use accessories of earth materials, such as clay, terra-cotta, and porcelain, in a bathroom located in the "heart" of your home.

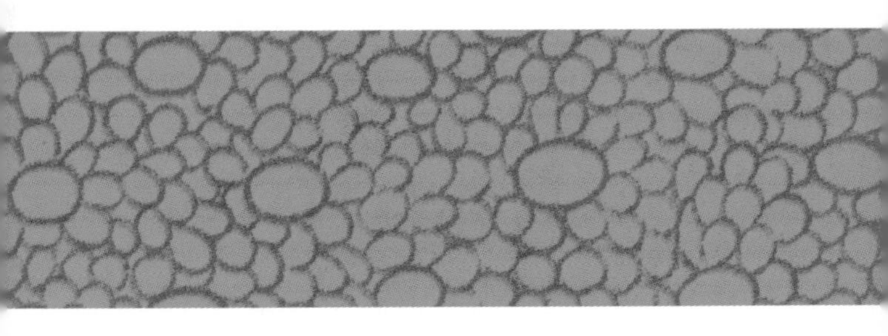

Don't locate a bathroom across from your kitchen—the yin energy of human waste is considered very detrimental to the financial and physical health of family members.

Do use a headboard on your bed to provide support for your crown chakra.

Don't place a bed with its foot facing the door, as this is very unlucky.

Do put your bed against a wall that doesn't have plumbing or a toilet on the other side.

Don't sleep in a bed that's located under a skylight, for this will draw healthy chi away from you.

Do place a symbol of wealth in your bedroom so that you see it upon waking each morning. This could be a figurine of a carp, an ox sitting on Chinese coins, or a turtle.

Do keep a pair of rose quartz (love) and red jasper (passion) hearts in the SW direction of your bedroom.

Don't store your exercise equipment in any part of your bed-room.

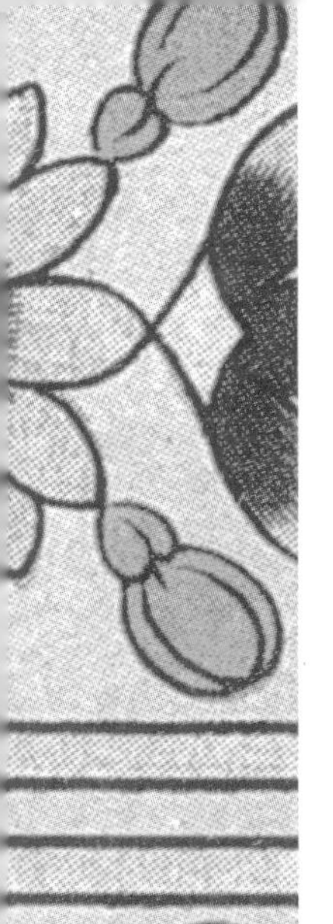

Do light beeswax candles in your bedroom before retiring to enhance your rest. They generate healthful ions into the air, while paraffin candles deplete the air of oxygen.

Do replace wilted flowers as soon as possible in a sick patient's room.

Don't sleep regularly in a basement bedroom, since being "underground" symbolizes being dead and buried!

Do remove all dead or dried flowers and plants from your bedroom (and garden), as they're believed to kill your love and sex life.

Do use soft, yin colors to decorate and accessorize your bedroom to help you sleep better. These include cream, along with cool pastels such as blues, grays, or greens.

Don't keep too much metal in your bedroom.

Do cover the television screen in your bedroom before you sleep.

Don't fill your bedroom with an overabundance of electronic gadgets and equipment, as they direct unhealthful sha energy toward your bed while you sleep.

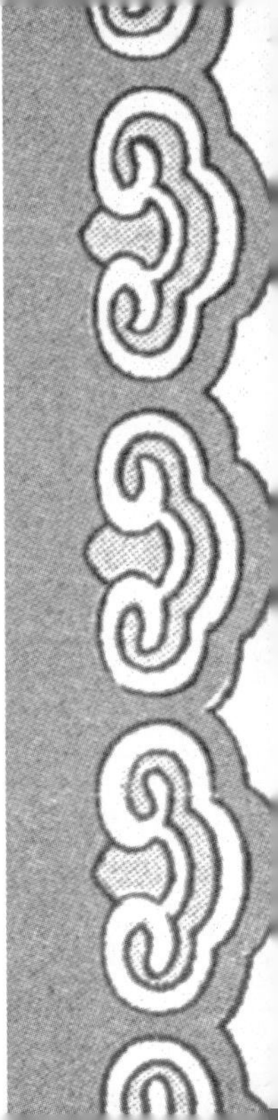

Do light pink (for love) and red (for passion) candles in the SW area of your bed-room and home.

Do smudge with lavender, or scent your bedroom with a lavender mist to promote a restful night's sleep.

Don't use the color peach in your bedroom if you're married, since it can cause infidelity.

Do sleep in bedrooms that are above the ground, rather than below, such as in a basement. Healthful yang energy is more abundant closer to light and fresh air.

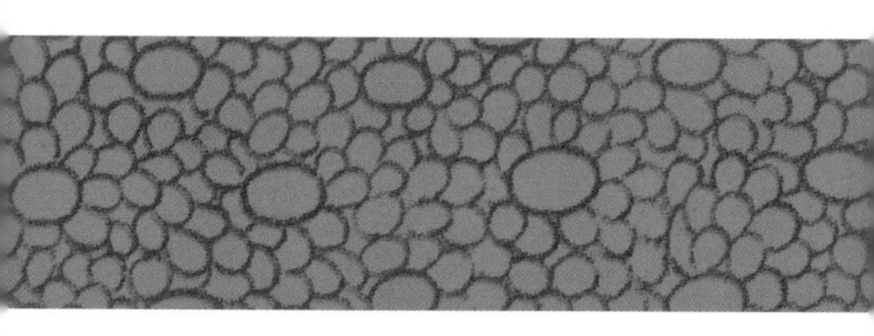

Do sleep in a bedroom that has a flat ceiling rather than one with odd angles, shapes, or windows that disturb the smooth flow of healthy chi.

Don't transform your bedroom into a greenhouse, as too many plants deprive you of healthful chi. Keeping one large plant or three small plants in the E for healthy benefits will suffice.

Do place a red cloth between the mattress and box spring for protection if you're sleeping in a bedroom above a garage.

Don't create a bed-room that's so fussy or feminine that it makes your male guests feel uncom-fortable being in it.

Do use a phoenix figurine in your bedroom to improve your relationship luck if you're single.

Don't decorate with too many masculine items if you're a single male—you don't want a woman to feel uncomfortable being in your home.

Do place peach, pink, or white fresh or silk peonies in a single woman's bedroom.

Don't fill your bed with pillows that would take the space of another person joining you there.

Do place two pink candles for love and romance in the SW area of a bachelorette's bedroom, as pink is a powerful color that stimulates relationships.

Do tie three bells with red ribbon and hang them on the inside doorknob of your main entrance to welcome prosperity into your home.

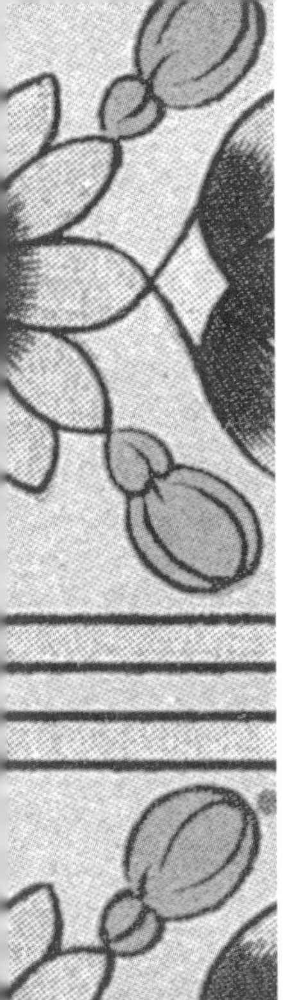

Don't keep antique bells recovered from religious buildings as accessories.

Do use tingshaw cymbals, a gong, or a brass bell with a handle to cleanse the energy of your home or office with sound during the fall season.

Don't bring temple or church bells into your home without first cleansing their energy by smudging.

Do put a statue, painting, or picture of a pair of birds—one male and one female—in the SW to enhance the romance energy of that area in your home.

Don't decorate your home or office with images of birds swooping down on their prey, as this may cause a takeover in your business.

Do place pictures of magpies or swallows in the S or SW—they symbolize good luck, good fortune, and happy news coming to a home.

Do put your self-help books in the N area of your room or home.

Do store your books about wealth, growth, and invest-ments in the SE.

Do position the spines of your books so that they're flush with the edges of open bookcase shelves.

Do keep the design and decor of your home and workplace functional and simple in order to facilitate a maximum chi flow and your good health.

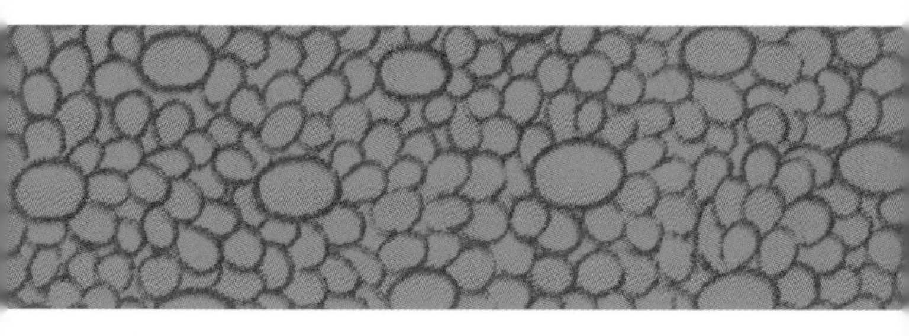

Don't block the main entrance to your home (called the "mouth of chi" in feng shui) with too much shrubbery or trees.

"Illness comes in by mouth, ills come out by it."

— Chinese proverb

Do keep your home and office free of clutter to facilitate clean chi flow. Doesn't your home feel great after you've tidied up in anticipation of company coming? You can capture and relive that feeling *every* day in a clutter-free environment.

Don't introduce purchases from flea markets, garage/estate sales, or failing businesses into your home or workplace unless you cleanse their energy first, since these items have absorbed the chi of the previous environment or occupants.

Do cleanse the energy as soon as possible after you entertain company in your home or your houseguests leave.

Do cleanse the energy of a new home or office before you move in so that you don't inherit any negative energy left from the previous occupants.

Do cleanse the energy in your home in the spring by misting every room with scented water.

Do remove and store out of sight all cleaning supplies after use so that they don't "clean out" your beneficial energy of prosperity and abundance.

Do an energy cleansing of your home during a new or full moon, which represents new beginnings.

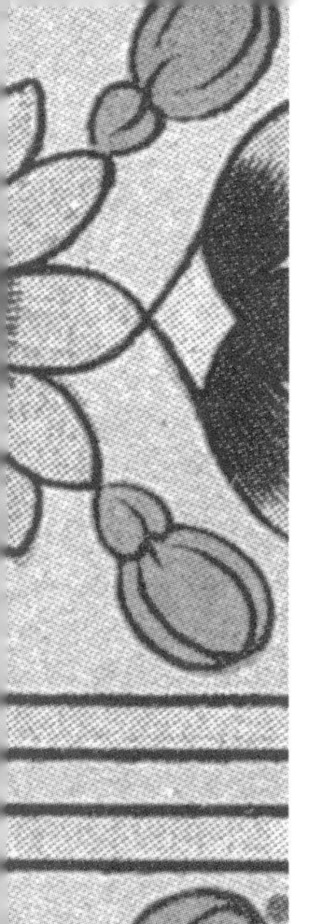

Don't bring collectors' items, such as historical (used) weaponry, swords, firearms, and so forth into your home without cleansing their energy first, as these items carry great negative yin energy.

Do an energy cleansing at your home and workplace if your energy and efforts are stagnating. Start by removing clutter, which slows down the flow of beneficial chi moving through your space.

Do energy cleanse with smudging, air, bells, singing bowls, music, clapping, or other methods on the day of the summer solstice, June 21, which is the most yang day of the year.

Do an energy cleansing in your home and office on September 21, the fall equinox.

Do an energy cleansing on December 22 before the upcoming holidays, and then again after your company leaves.

Do use red ribbon to string three Chinese coins together through their square center holes, and dangle them on the inside door-knob of your home or office to welcome abun-dance in.

Do hang a strand of eight Chinese coins in the N, NW, or W area of your office for enhanced prosperity.

Do use the shape of coins in the W, as metal is made into circles and represents financial success.

Do enclose three Chinese or silver coins in a lucky red envelope and tape it under your phone, fax machine, or cash register to stimulate money luck. (The numbers three, six, and nine are a powerful combination in Chinese culture and in feng shui.)

Do fashion your own unique pendants, bracelets, and other jewelry with Chinese coins. Wear the bracelet on your left (yang) wrist to stimulate money luck.

Do add blue or yellow to your bedroom if you're experiencing infertility.

Do use aquamarine in the N to activate the water element of this direction, representing business success and career growth.

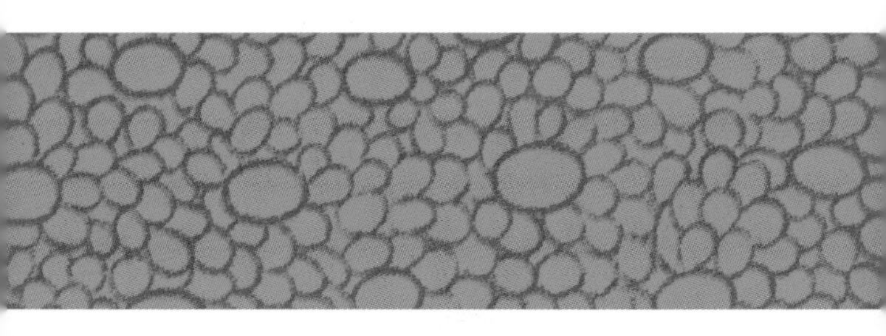

Don't put any blue or black in the S, which governs the fire element in your home and represents happiness.

Do remove the color green from your environment if you're feeling a lot of anger.

Do use a lot of yellow, the color of the element of earth, to "dam" the outflow of water (prosperity) if a bathroom is at the center of your home or office space.

Don't create an imbalance of yellow in your home—too much of any earth color may cause you to worry excessively.

Do add more blue to the N areas of your home if you're experiencing low levels of sexual energy or interest, as this could indicate a water deficiency.

Do represent autumn during that season with gold (earth) colors, which generate metal (symbolizing the abundance of harvest).

Don't have too many yang colors such as yellow, orange, or red in your bedroom—they're too stimulating.

Do adorn your bedroom in soft, dark, passive, nurturing yin colors (think of a cool stream flowing through a forest), as these colors are much more conducive to regenerating your mind, body, and spirit during your sleep at night.

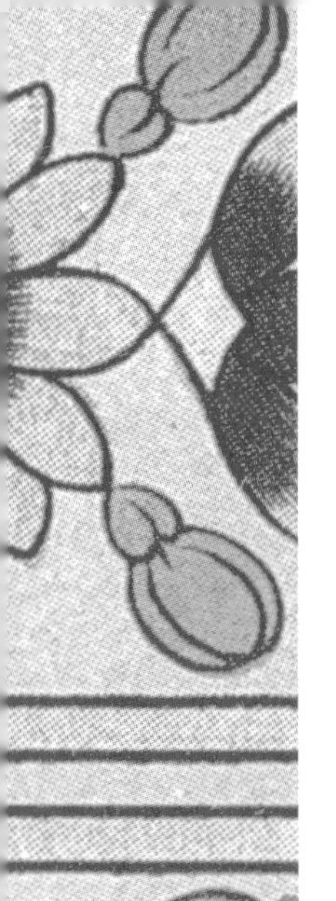

Do use the colors of the ocean and the sky in the NE to activate the energy of those who are studying in your home.

Don't add the fire element orange to the water area of N.

Do paint your SW bedroom wall yellow if you want to become a mother.

Do cool down if the yang energy of the summer is too intense for you by surrounding yourself with, and wearing more, sea-foam green and aqua blue.

Don't use too much green or blue to decorate the heart of your home, as these colors represent wood and water and weaken the center.

Do use the color orange in the S (fire) or SW (earth).

Do paint your kitchen walls with light, pastel colors to bring lots of yang energy in for good digestion and health.

Don't decorate your kitchen in dark colors because it's the source of yang in your home, where life-giving energy is created with proper food and diet.

Do hang a picture of peach-colored peonies either on the inside or outside wall of an unmarried daughter's bedroom to help her find the right kind of man.

Do add the color red throughout your home to increase joy and happiness.

Do use your compass, which the Chinese invented for the proper situating of graves, to show a family's honor and respect to its deceased.

"Heaven lent you a soul. Earth will lend you a grave."
— Chinese proverb

Do place your computer in the right direction to achieve your goals—the N activates creativity, while the SE generates income.

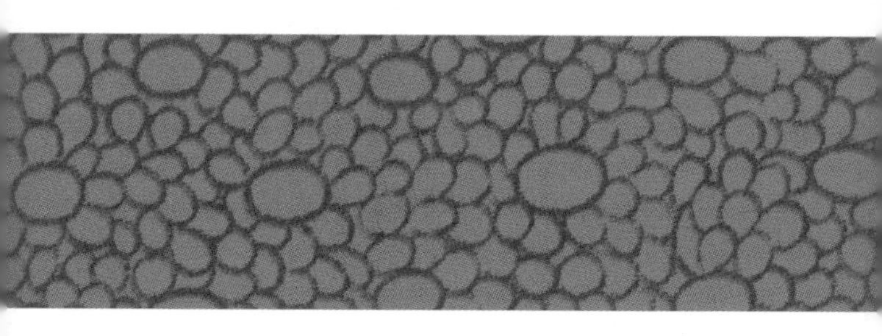

Do wear jewelry with fluorite, tourmaline, onyx, or tiger-eye beads to help you maintain balance while studying or working on your computer.

Do keep heart-shaped stones and crystals in your romance and love corner.

Do place any faceted crystal figurine on a windowsill to disperse the killing energy of a lamppost or corner of a neighboring building.

Do remove the energy of people who have touched your crystals by gently washing them with a sea-salt solution. Dry by turning the crystals upside down and allowing the water to drip away.

Don't forget to keep your colored crystals out of the sun, as they'll fade. Only white or clear crystals can be activated in sunny spots.

Do wear crystals with prosperity-enhancing properties—these include citrine, ametrine, adven-turine, black onyx, jade, and coral.

Do install a sparkling citrine or ametrine crystal on or above your telephone, computer, or fax machine to generate more business.

Do reenergize your crystals by dusting them once in a while and putting them outdoors to recharge by the light of a full moon.

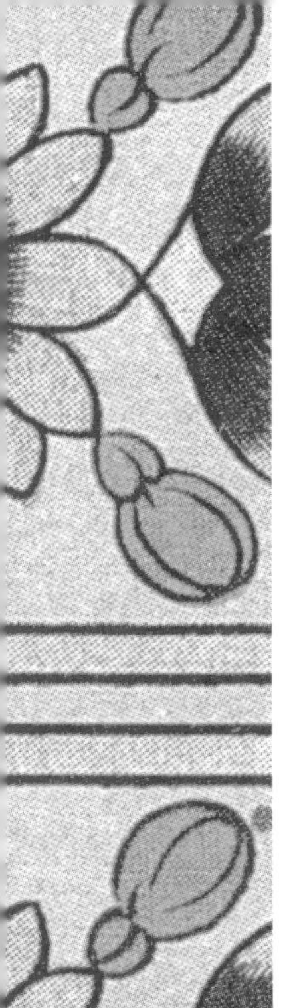

Do add a statue of a wish-fulfilling cow to the outside E or SE corner of your desk.

Do have a wall behind your desk so that you'll always enjoy solid support for your business endeavors.

Don't locate a work surface under heavy light, air-conditioning ducts, pipes, or any sort of beams, as these will push energy down on you and cause work difficulties and headaches.

Do match the material of your work surface with the compass direction in which it's located: wood in the S and SE; metal or stone in the W, NW, and N; and so on.

Do notice that those who sit with their backs to the door in a meeting or conference room have less influence.

Don't place your desk under a beam, which will give you a feeling of energy pressing down on you and your work, depleting your vitality.

Do put a heavy object (not your overflowing in-box!) on the outside corner of your desk closest to the door.

"Customers are jade. Merchandise is grass."
— Chinese proverb

Do remember that a major component of your destiny is charity and philanthropy, so volunteer your time and resources to benefit your community.

"If you don't have charity, you have the worst kind of heart trouble."

— Bob Hope

Do create good karma with your donations of belongings that you no longer need or use. This is a way to manifest charity and philanthropy.

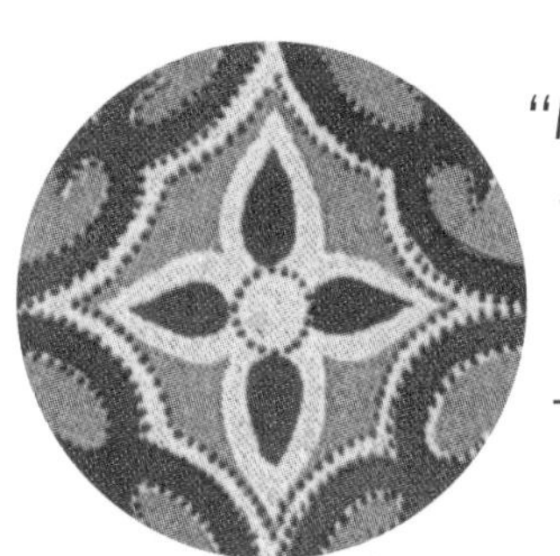

"If you always give, you will always have."
— Chinese proverb

Do engender good karma through random acts of love and kindness without thought of reciprocation or reward. You're contributing to good human luck, one of the critical components of your destiny.

Do keep in mind that each one of us creates our own destiny through our thoughts, words, and deeds. Everything that happens to us is a consequence of a choice or decision we made in the past.

"Better to be kind at home than burn incense far away."
— Chinese proverb

Do show your thanks for life and its many gifts by collecting and donating your unused clothing and household items to charity. Doing so creates good human-made luck for yourself and your family.

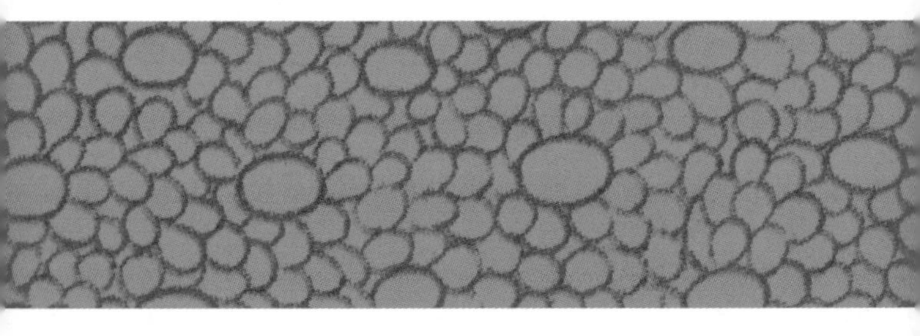

Do hang a mirror on the W wall of your dining room to multiply the reflection of lots of food and drink on your table.

Do decorate with an image of abundant food, fruit, wine, and so on in a painting, sculpture, or picture on your dining room wall.

Do have a nook for your family meals rather than eating in a "great room" where there's a conflict of yin (quiet) and yang (active) activities.

Do have a solid wood or metal

door at your main entrance,

since it will provide protection

and support for your family.

Do use a wood door if the entrance to your home faces E, SE, or S.

Don't install a door that's more than a third glass—it permits the beneficial chi and wealth to flow out.

Do use a metal door if your front door faces W, NW, or N.

Don't locate the powder room past the front door if you're remodeling your home, since to do so represents your family's prosperity exiting.

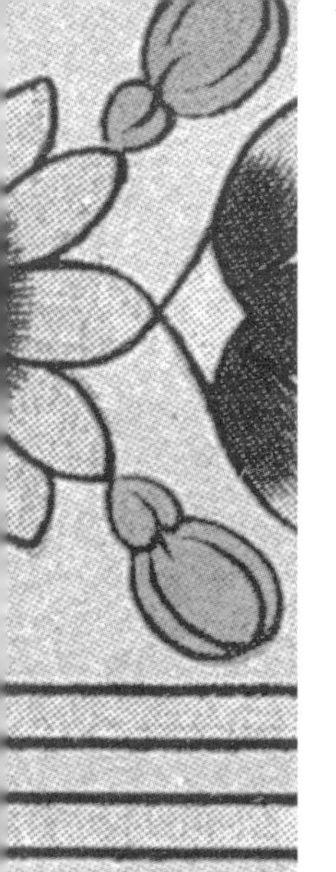

Do polish your metal door knocker to deflect negative energy directed at your home from a straight driveway.

Don't use all-glass doors in your main entrance. These facilitate a fast passage of beneficial chi and wealth from your home, rushing through so as not to allow their blessings to remain in your family.

Do install small beveled windows in your wooden doors, or sidelights on each side of them.

Don't have a kitchen door that opens inward. Food that's prepared there symbolizes good health and nutrition and should be honored with a door leading out to the dining room.

Don't keep a dragon image next to the ashes of a person or pet.

Do position your dragon pictures and statues in a lively, busy area of your home, such as the great or family room—preferably in the E to activate wealth, good health, and harmony.

Don't place a dragon figurine or image near a cremation urn if it's stored in your home—to do so may adversely affect your good fortune because ashes of the deceased are very yin.

Don't put a dragon figurine in your kitchen. It's better to have it in your office to enhance your career.

Do add more stones and crystals to your environment if you crave sweets—you have an earth deficiency.

Do use a gate with rectangles or squares in its design in the earth directions of NE or SW.

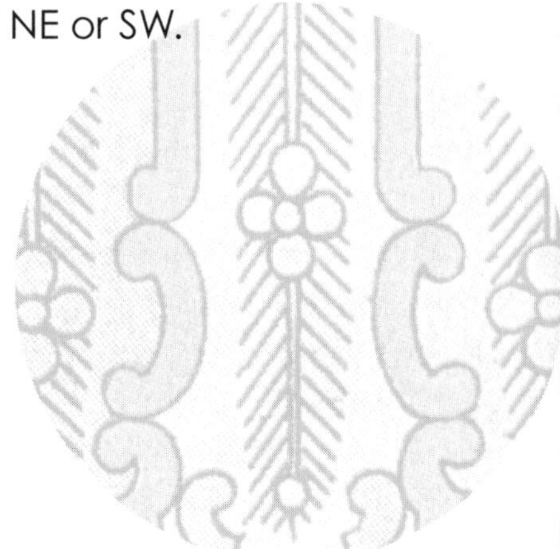

Don't employ too many crystals or stones in your decorating, as digestive disorders are caused by too much of the earth element.

Do place at least one large stone, ceramic, or porcelain item in the center of your home to anchor its "heart."

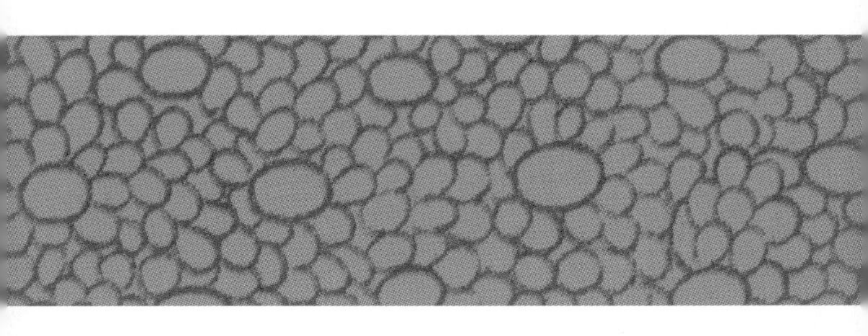

Do represent the earth element in your kitchen with clay, terracotta, porcelain, marble, granite, stone, and china accessories.

Do have a wooden bowl filled with dried lotus seeds in the E (family) area of your bedroom, as lotus seeds mean "continual children."

Do stimulate good health and money luck by putting a prosperity-bamboo plant growing in water in your dining or living room if it's located in the E area of your home.

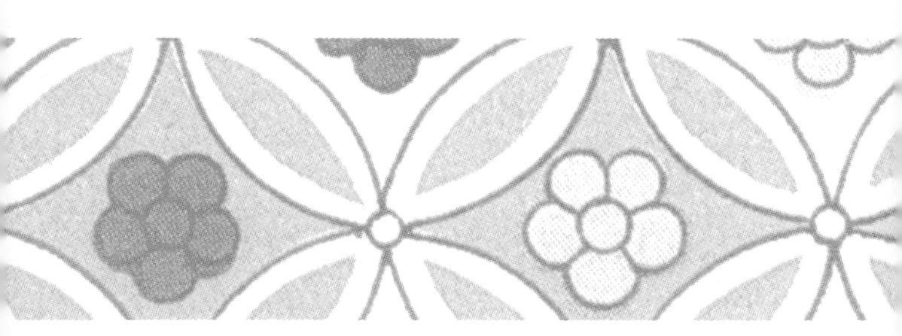

Do keep a bowl of fruit, especially oranges or tangerines (representing gold) in the E corner of your kitchen or dining room.

Do keep a wooden elephant in the E or SE as a fertility symbol. (Be sure to choose one that has its trunk raised up.)

Do avoid using harmony- and health-destroying metal in any E area of your home or bedroom.

Do remove the metal exercise equipment and television from your bedroom, especially in the E, as they disturb your health energy.

Don't keep a lot of metal objects

or too much electronic equipment

in the E area of your

family room.

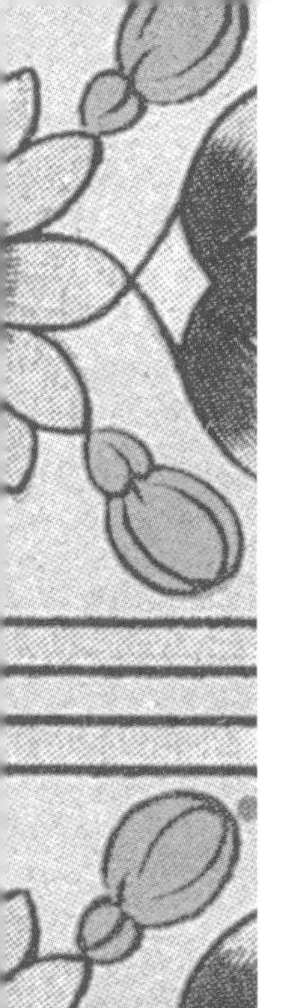

Do decorate with blue and green in the E and SE for harmony, wealth, and good health.

Do avoid placing metal furniture in the E, as the metal element will destroy the beneficial wood of this direction, representing harmony, fortune, and good health.

Do put a wooden statue of a dragon or *Kwan Yin,* the goddess of family, in the E to maintain harmony and cooperation in your home.

Do decorate with natural fibers such as cotton, linen, and silk in your home for good health.

Don't use too many synthetic fabrics in your home, as these emanate sha energy in the form of toxic gases and odors that are detrimental to your health.

Do install your ceiling fans beyond the foot of a bed in a bedroom—they'll still cool the room without harming the health of the occupants.

Do use a handheld fan or small compact mirror to deflect the negative energy emanating from somebody or something.

Do remember that no home or office enjoys perfect feng shui all the time. Because the universe is always in a state of change, so are the energies around us.

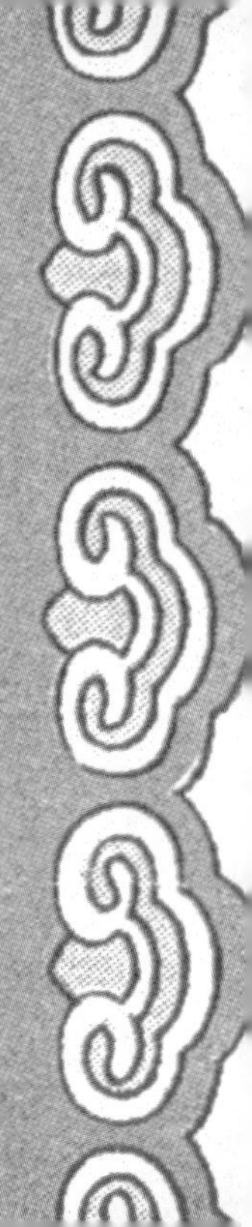

Do keep a feng shui diary to record your efforts and the results that follow.

Do introduce yin energy into your home or office with cooler, darker colors; and images of pools, lakes, forests, and rivers.

Do bring yang energy into your home or office with bright, vibrant colors; images and artwork of mountains; moving objects; and light.

Do make only minor feng shui adjustments if you're reasonably happy, healthy, financially secure, and in harmony with those around you.

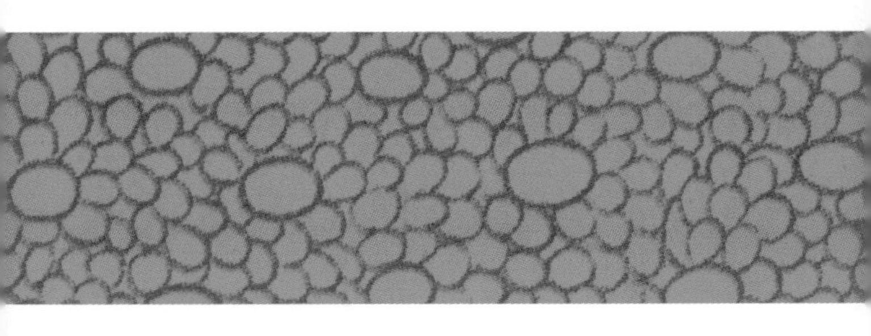

Do use one of the following techniques to mitigate or correct a feng shui challenge: hide it, camouflage it, bury it, block it, reflect it, deflect it, remove it, or divert it.

Do remember the 3rd Golden Rule of the Feng Shui Lady: *Everything is fixable*. Feng shui empowers you and lets you take charge of your environment to transform your life through the appropriate use of C(olor), A(nimal symbol), N(umber) and E(lement).

Do keep in mind that those who practice feng shui with good character, faith in themselves, and an open heart and mind get results.

"'I heard' is good. 'I saw' is better. 'I did' is to understand." — Chinese proverb

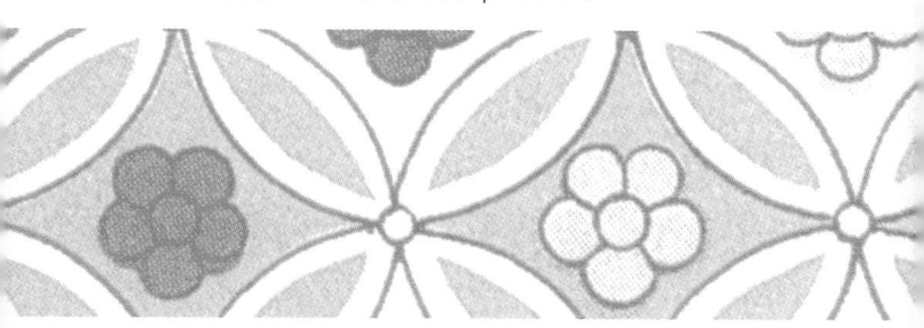

Do know that feng shui parallels life: light and dark, hard and soft, active and passive, straight and crooked—all are complementary and interdependent halves of a holistic philosophy that centers and empowers us all.

Do have fun collecting fertility symbols from around the world to activate parenthood in your home if you're planning on a family this year.

Do put a fertility symbol of earth materials to activate motherhood in the SW.

Do give six pairs of chopsticks tied with red ribbon for a fun wedding gift, as chopsticks represent "continuing children" and are a fertility symbol in Chinese culture.

Do place a metal fertility statue to activate fatherhood energy in the NW.

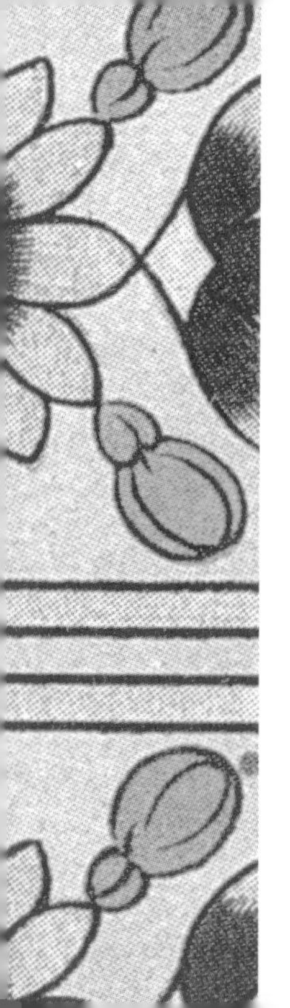

Do use the element of fire in your home if you want to feel more easygoing and relaxed.

Do add more candles or lights to your home if you stammer or have speech difficulties.

Do burn soy, palm, food-grade, or beeswax candles in your home for good health. These are natural ingredients that won't put soot into the air.

Don't put lamps or candles in the W or NW metal directions, as the fire element destroys the metal.

Do add the element of fire to your kitchen with candles, pyramid shapes, and a little bit of the color red.

Do put silver- or black-colored angel fish or mollies (tropical aquarium fish) in a glass-and-metal tank.

Do place fresh or silk peonies in a vase in the SW area of your bedroom if you're a single woman. The peony is the symbol of love in Chinese culture, just as the rose is in the West.

Do increase healthful and healing yang energy in a sick person's bedroom with the presence of fresh flowers.

Do put a white or yellow orchid plant in a metallic vase in the W area of your bedroom if you're interested in many offspring.

Do give the gift of a narcissus plant (to put in the E or SE) to wish good fortune to the recipient.

Do sit at round or oval tables to enjoy your meals and promote harmony with your family.

Do add the colors of the elements to each meal: red, yellow, green, blue (corn), black (beans), and white.

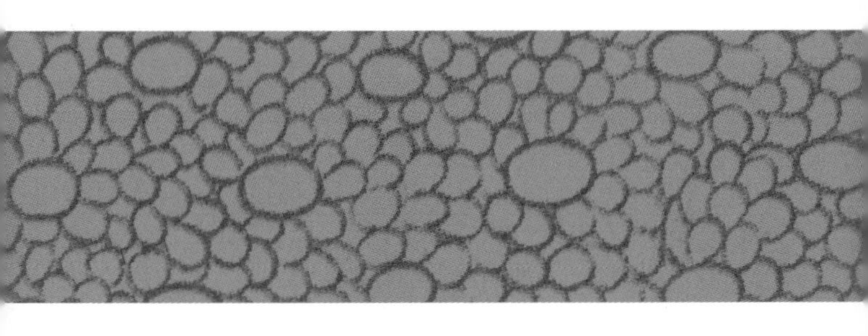

Do close your business early on the afternoon of the winter solstice, December 21, so that families can enjoy their evening meal together.

Do maintain a balanced diet of yang (animal) and yin (plant).

Do eat cleansing foods such as soups and smoothies in the spring; lots of fruits and vegetables in the summer to counter its heat; sweet, savory foods in the autumn; and hot, spicy foods in the winter to speed up your metabolism. The Chinese believe that good diet, exercise, and nutrition are the keys to a long life.

Do notice that in Chinese decor, there's a minimal amount of furniture and accessories. This spaciousness allows the cosmic energy of chi to move freely throughout.

Do use furnishings crafted from marble, stone, or granite in your home if you have dry or cracked lips and feel thirsty often.

Don't acquire a piece of furniture, no matter how good a deal you may get, from a failed or corrupt business—you'll inherit the negative energy of its former owner and environment.

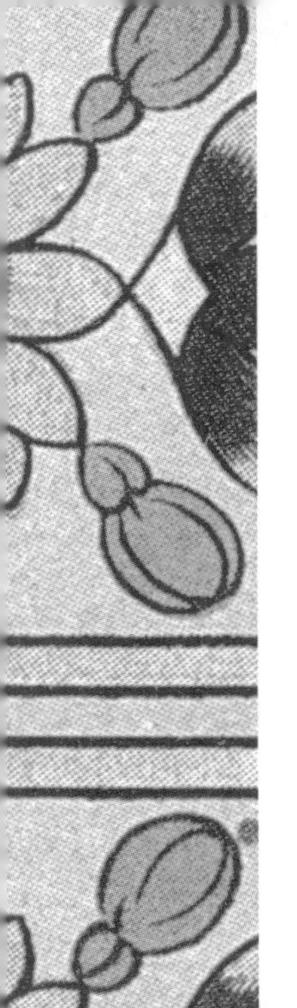

Do position a heavy cabinet or bed first in the S area of your new house, apartment, or condo.

Do add pyramid and pointed shapes to the S part of your garden to represent its element of fire.

Do keep a garden that has a good balance of sun and shade, or yang and yin energies.

Do make your garden feng shui compliant; after all, Chinese gardens are designed to represent a microcosm of the universe.

Do include many pine trees in your land-scaping and garden, as the Chinese believe that they promote long life and good health by generating much healthful chi into the air.

Don't locate your metal toolshed in the E (wood, wealth) area of your garden.

Do incorporate straight lines (yang) and curves (ying) when planning your garden paths. Chinese gardens resemble natural English gardens more than their formal European counterparts.

Do prune the leaves of trees and shrubbery so that they don't touch the walls of a house, thus drawing the energy away from it.

Do generate lots of oxygen into the air through the place-ment of pine trees in your yard.

Do thin out the thick foliage of your property's trees so that the sun and its yang energy can permeate your garden and your life.

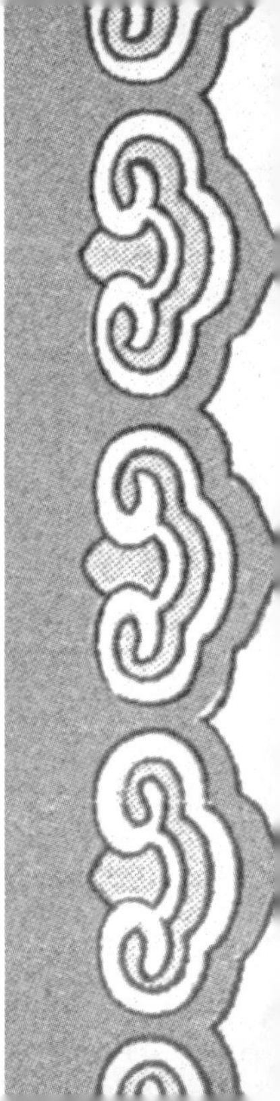

Don't remove a healthy tree—if you simply must do so, plant three others to replace its life and spirit.

Do step into your feng shui garden often—and be sure to create new views, delightful surprises, or spots of beauty whenever you can.

Do use a color wheel to harmonize your garden's plants and blooms so that they complement each other.

Do locate gazebos and cupolas with pointed roofs, which represent fire, in the S, SW, or NE area of your garden.

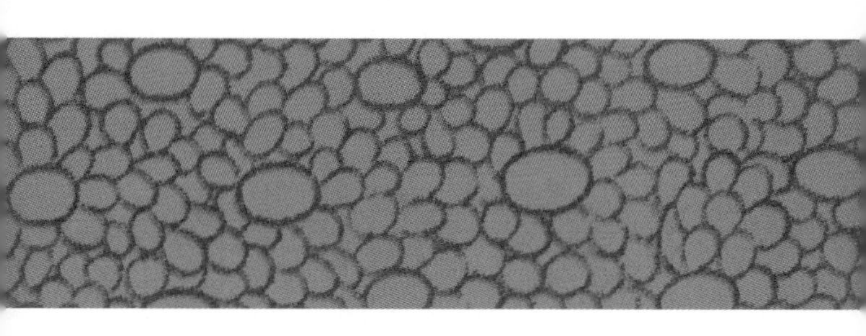

Don't disturb any natural object or formation that has medicinal benefits, such as a mineral spring or a sacred tree. A garden kept close to its natural state has the best feng shui.

Do take great care of, and cherish anything on, your property that has been identified as possessing sacred or restorative powers.

Do use odd (yang) numbers when grouping plants together in your garden.

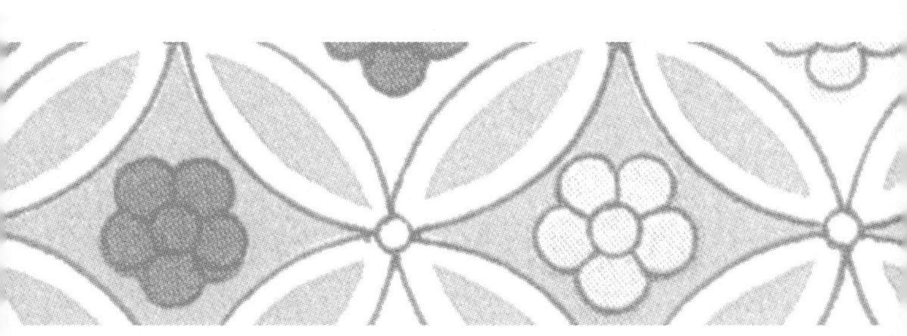

Do create a cozy, romantic spot for you and your partner in the SW area of your garden, adding heart shapes, stones, a marble statue, or other accessories in twos.

Do endeavor to transform your garden into a place of healing, solitude, and peace; as well as one for family activities, active sports, and socializing. Always try to maintain the balance of yin and yang, just as in life.

Don't give a clock as a gift, for it symbolizes the quick passage of time and a shortened life.

Do fold dollar bills into creative shapes and string them together to make a lei of good wishes and good fortune for a newlywed couple or birthday honoree.

Don't give sharp objects as gifts to anyone, as these symbolize the severance of a friendship or a life.

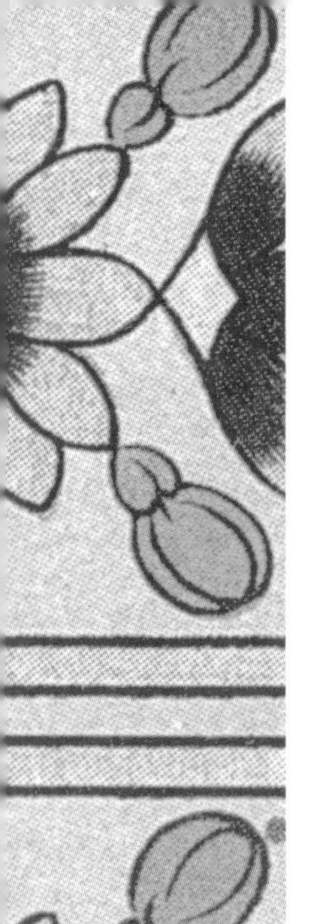

Do choose a gravesite with good feng shui attributes for your parents and grandparents, and you'll enjoy many blessings in life.

Don't neglect the care and maintenance of your ancestors' burial sites. Feng shui practices originated from the careful and proper orientation of those family graves belonging to members who preceded the living.

Do keep your emotions, environment, and lifestyle in balance—the Chinese believe that disruption of these three are the reasons for disease.

Do create and enjoy a cozy, relaxing spot in your home to boost your liver functions.

Do hang wood and water scenes on the walls in the directions of E and S, which are associated with good health and harmony in the home and office.

Do put wood accessories in the E to stimulate good health and well-being.

Do continue to live in the home in which your children were conceived or born. It has the auspicious *ling* particles of fertility, as well as life's chi energy.

Don't use an excess of wood or water as decoration in the center of your home. The element of wood destroys earth, which should be at the heart of the home.

Do spend more of your decorating budget on the critical rooms of your home (kitchen, master bedroom, and home office), rather than your bathrooms.

Don't select a home with a spiral staircase, toilet, or skylight at its center.

Do choose a home that's situated on the inside curve of a road or waterway. This configuration is very lucky, as you're being "hugged" by wealth!

Do wear your birthstone or other beneficial gemstones to protect yourself from absorbing other people's energy.

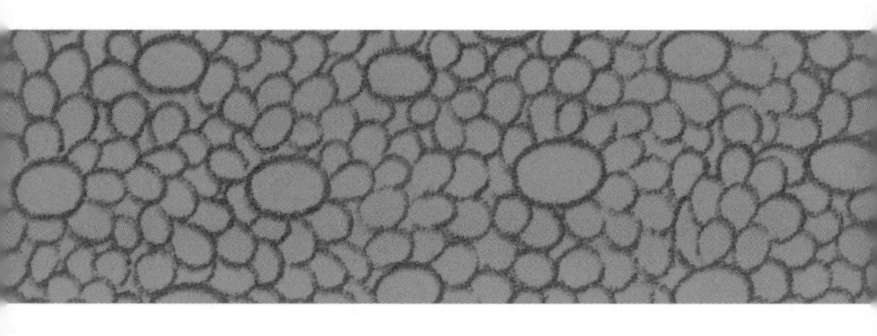

Do regularly clean your gem-stone jewelry to remove any negative energy it has absorbed from the people you come in contact with.

Do combine Chinese coins—which are ideal for wearing as jewelry, especially worn on your left (yang) wrist—with doughnut-shaped jade pieces to activate money luck.

Do keep your kitchen, which is the area where yang energy originates, bright, clean, well lit, and well ventilated.

Do add the water element to your kitchen in the form of glass, tea, coffee, fruit juices, and other beverages; as well as in cooking, washing, and cleaning activities.

Don't install too much metal in your kitchen. Lots of stainless steel (such as the stove, refrigerator, sink, and ovens) causes an imbalance of this element, which destroys the healthful wood represented by fruits and vegetables.

Do design your kitchen to include all five elements: wood, fire, earth, metal, and water.

Do wash your dishes in a sink that has a window above it, thus infusing healthful yang energy into them.

Don't clutter your kitchen countertops with utensils and decorative objects, as these slow down the flow of beneficial chi.

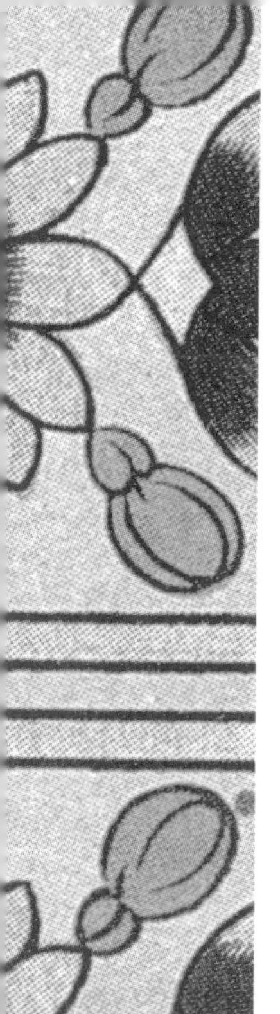

Do stow the garbage can out of sight in your kitchen.

Do put away any supplies used in cleaning after their use in the dining room or kitchen.

Don't take your meals regularly at a counter, especially if you sit on a stool, as there is no support for you.

Do keep your kitchen simple in design, and maintain uncluttered counters.

Don't locate your kitchen next to a bedroom.

Do store your knives out of sight in a drawer or cabinet to minimize family friction.

Don't paint your kitchen walls a dark color or cover them with dark wallpaper. This brings too much yin energy to an important yang room where food creates energy and sustains life.

Do place a ceramic pitcher or fruit bowl between the stove and the sink in a galley kitchen. This prevents the water element from extinguishing the fire element (prosperity).

Don't locate your kitchen next to the living room.

Do put wooden kitchen utensils in the E, SE, or S, and metal items like pots and pans in the W, NW, or N.

Don't keep a "dirty kitchen" (or a smaller kitchen for frying food), as this represents a division of your family's finances.

Do stimulate the yang energy of your kitchen with the use of natural and artificial light, and bright, cheerful colors on the walls.

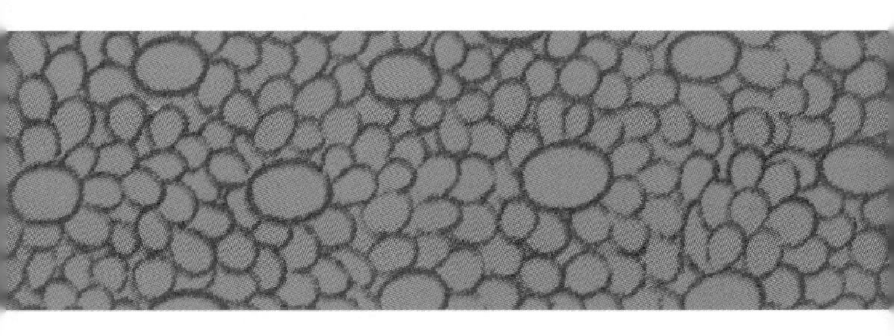

Don't cover your kitchen walls with dark-colored paint or wallpaper, as it needs to be a place of light energy to activate good health.

Do tuck a red envelope with three Chinese coins into the bottom of the rice or potato storage bin for abundance and wealth.

Do add more metal accessories to your home (but not in the bedroom) if you have problems with asthma, wheezing, or shortness of breath—all of which could indicate a deficiency in the metal element.

Do place seven pictures of children in silver, copper, pewter, or other metal frames in the W to improve your offspring luck.

Do bring the metal element into your kitchen through pots, pans, bowls, small appliances, utensils, and tools.

Do place a metal figure of children to stimulate fertility energy in the W.

Don't use metal containers to store food, as this element changes composition when it rusts.

Do add more metal in the form of copper, silver, brass, or pewter in your home if your skin is dry and flaky.

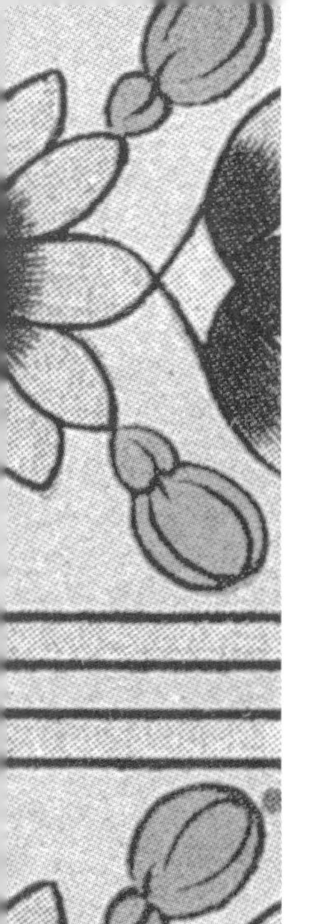

Do nourish your lungs with confidence by adding metal sculptures or figurines in active, yang rooms.

Do use white, silver, gold, bronze, and copper objects in the W to stimulate your son or daughter's fame.

Do hang a simple round mirror (facing out) on a suction hook on a window to reflect back negative sha, or "killing," energy caused by the sight of a Dumpster, lamp-post, or neighboring home's gable.

Do bounce light back with a simple mirror set in the window track facing out—since, as a rule of thumb, any building or room that's illuminated by the head-lights of vehicles at night is getting an unhealthy dose of adverse sha energy.

Do position a standard red, green, and gold octagonal bagua mirror to face a trouble-some neighbor's door or window to send his or her negative energy back—don't be surprised if they move away!

Don't embellish your bagua mirror with arrowheads or other pointed objects that are harmful to others, as this will create bad karma for yourself.

Do employ a bagua mirror prudently: Only hang it on the exterior of your home or right up against window glass with its back facing into the room.

MIRROR

Do use tortoise shells and gongs, like the Chinese, or silver or pewter plates on plate stands instead of mirrors to deflect negative sha energy.

Don't hang the powerful bagua mirror surrounded by the trigrams anywhere *inside* your home.

Don't allow the trunk of a tree or a lamppost to obstruct your perception of the world from the entrance to your home. Hang a small round mirror above your front door or under an eave to deflect either view.

Do put your curvy metal gate or fence in the N.

Do work in the N area of a well-lit room if you're feeling creative or want to stimulate your imagination.

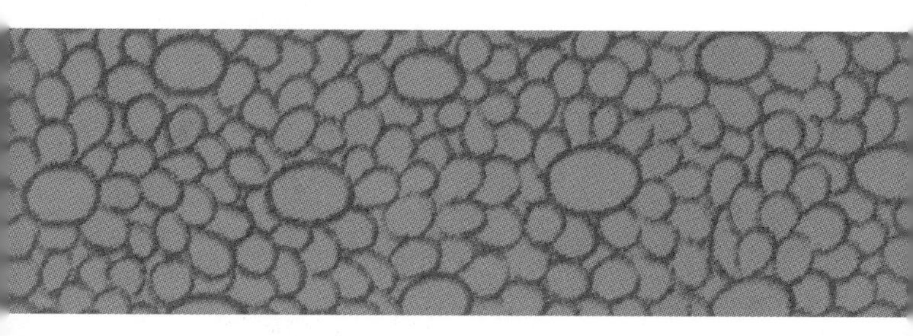

Do locate your success library in the N if you want to be inspired and motivated.

Do use a black, white, or gray-colored metal gate in the N.

Do keep an elephant statue in the N, and rub its forehead often to activate the children luck in your home.

Do enhance the NE area with earth materials for knowledge and self-cultivation.

"If you rest, you rust!"
— Helen Hayes

Do place fluorite or tiger-eye crystals or figurines in the NE to help you focus on your studies.

NORTHEAST

Do study in an NE room (or one that's facing NE) for academic luck.

"Gold has its price. Learning is beyond price." — Chinese proverb.

Do hunker down to surf the Net, read a book, or learn something new and challenging in the NE.

Do study in the NE area of your home or bedroom to do well in your academic endeavors.

"Food cures hunger. Study cures ignorance."

— Chinese proverb

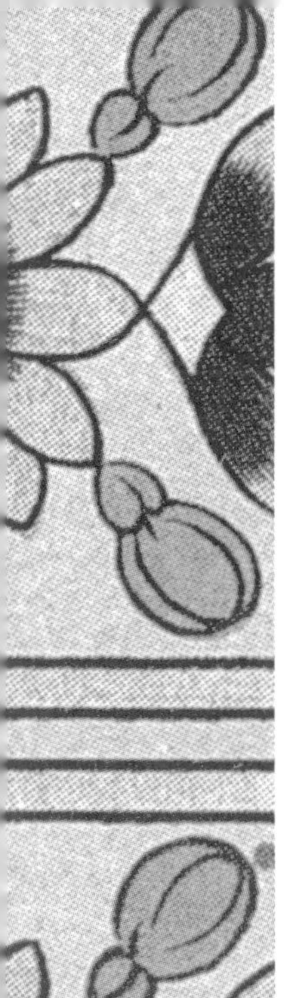

Do place a pagoda wind chime outside in the NW.

Do maintain a grove of trees in the NW area of your garden or yard to maintain protection for your family.

Do hang a framed travel poster of a dream destination on the NW wall of a room.

Do keep your outdoor statue of the Virgin Mary or Buddha (raised off the ground) in the supporting energy of the NW.

Do paint your NW bedroom wall either white or gray, which represents fatherhood.

Do put six items collected from your travels in the NW area of your library or study.

Do retain hills and trees anywhere in the NW zone of your lot, thus supporting the male head of household.

Do put ceramic figurines representing your favorite travel location in the NW area of your family room.

Do nourish your heart with lots of love and beauty in your home and office.

Do move your desk out from under any overhead architectural features, such as pipes, ducts, or beams, which will adversely affect your focus and concentration.

Don't choose a desk or office at the end of a long hallway or corridor, as you'll absorb much killing sha energy created by the straight line, and experience illness and bad luck.

Do place a large natural citrine, amethyst, or ametrine crystal on the outside corner of your desk, near your office's entrance.

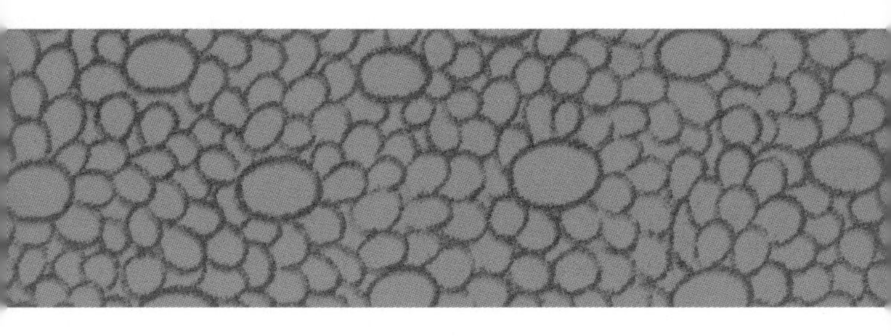

Do use the appropriate colors on your desktop, according to the direction where you're sitting in your office: green and brown for S, E, and SE; white or metallics for W, NW, and N.

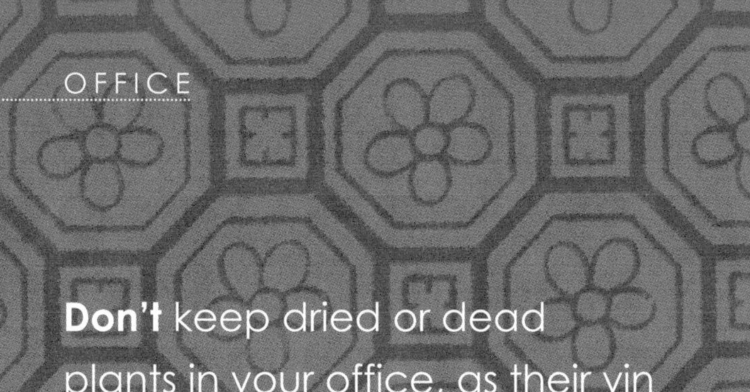

Don't keep dried or dead plants in your office, as their yin energy will negatively affect your business prospects.

Do display your awards and certificates on the S wall of your office to symbolize your achievements.

Do arrive at a meeting early so that you can choose the command position in the room, which is located diagonally across from the entrance.

Don't sit with your back to the room in any crucial meetings or negotiations, as this will weaken your power, influence, and position.

Do keep a single silver arowana fish in the office aquarium to generate business. (Notice them at Chinese restaurants for the same reason!)

Do place a stone figurine or crystal on the sill if there's a window behind your desk to simulate a mountain for support.

Don't activate the romance energies in your place of business—it's
unwise to mix your personal and
professional lives there.

Do anchor the wealth and success of your business by positioning your safe in the W, the NW, or especially the N.

Do store your business files away from the bathroom or toilet.

Don't sit behind a hinged door

in your office or at a meeting.

Do place a faceted crystal or glass candy dish or vase on your desk in line with the hall-way to deflect direct, killing sha energy if your office is at the end of a corridor—other-wise, your energy, health, and concentration may suffer.

Do use the image of a phoenix in your home to add spark in an existing relationship if it's stagnant.

Don't use a phoenix to activate romance in your life if you already have a happy, satisfying relationship (both emotionally and physically) with someone special—to do so may attract infidelity.

Don't place the image of a phoenix next to the right side of your front door, as you may be activating "other woman" energy into your household.

Don't place the phoenix image in a child's bedroom.

Do place a vase of prosperity bamboo by your front door if it's located in the NW.

Do understand that while lots of flowers and plants in your home generate active yang energy, they should be kept to a minimum in your bedroom, which should be more yin.

Don't keep too many cacti with thorns or sharp points inside your home, as they cre-ate harmful sha energy.

Do accessorize your home with plants that have rounded, not sharp or spiked, leaves or foliage.

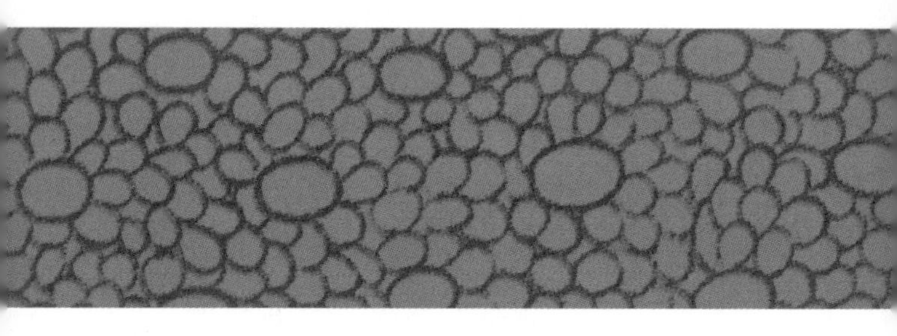

Do keep lots of healthy green plants in your family room to keep the peace when everyone assembles there.

Do plan your garden pond, designing and situating it so that the sun shines on its surface.

Do position large boulders (yang) sticking out of your pond's water (yin) to create the balance of hard and soft.

Do keep in mind that turtles are very lucky, so duplicate ancient imperial Chinese gardens by putting your turtle-filled pond in the N, E, or SE.

Do place a salt lamp in the E or S part of the room of an ill family member to pump more negative ions into the air, thus promoting faster healing.

Do purify the energy of your home after your spring cleaning by tossing a pinch of sea salt into its corners.

Do your daily meditation facing the S or E to nourish both your mind and soul.

Do plant a matching set of red flowers for family protection on each side of your front door if it faces S.

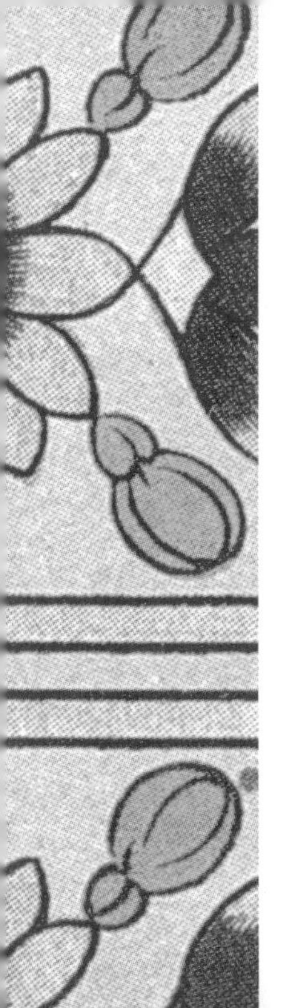

Do place your books about, pictures of and with, and autographed items from, celebrities in the fame and money area of S.

Don't place waterfalls or tabletop fountains in the S area of a room or office—to do so symbolizes water extinguishing fire, which stands for fame and fortune.

Do liberally use a shade of red in the S to enhance happiness, fortune, long life, and protection.

Do plant cone-shaped trees in the S part of your garden to match its fire element.

Don't have a window in the S wall of your kitchen, as it's too yang.

Don't put a water element such as a pond or fountain in the S part of your yard or inside your home, as the water extinguishes the beneficial properties of fire: long life, fortune, joy, and opportunity.

Do bring in and place a heavy piece of furniture into the S first when you move into your new home, as it will "ground" your family. When you're ready to sell your house, move that piece away from that spot.

Do add red, pink, orange, or purple flowering plants to your landscaping in the S.

Do put a picture or statue of a Chinese emperor's eight galloping horses in the S area of

your home or office.

Do add the colors of green and purple to the SE area of your living room to stimulate the money energy of the family.

Don't store your metal tools and equipment in the SE if you develop any plants for competition or prizes.

Do group a pair of porcelain or stone elephants in the SW area of your bedroom to activate the children energy there.

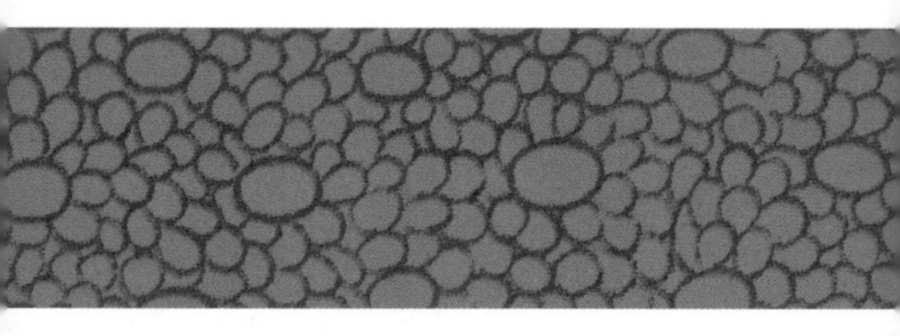

Do use yellows and golds in the earth direction of SW.

Do add fire elements—such as lights, firepits, barbeques, and tiki torches—to add extra punch to the SW relationship area of your property, garden, or yard.

Do create a romance corner with photos of happily married couples and love motifs such as hearts and flowers in the SW area of your bedroom (which should also be clear of clutter). This area is conducive to good relationships.

Don't put wood items such as benches, lattices, or gates in the SW portion of your garden, as they will destroy the benefits of this area: relationships, marriage, love, and motherhood.

Do decorate with candles in multiples of two in the SW area of your bedroom.

Do tie two red ribbons on the inside doorknob of your bedroom door if it is located in the SW, and keep the door closed except when in use.

Do add symbols and images of mother and child to the SW area of your bedroom.

Do enhance relationships in your life by adding two red, white, or pink candles to the SW area of your bedroom or home.

"Hide your offended heart, keep your valued friend."

— Chinese proverb

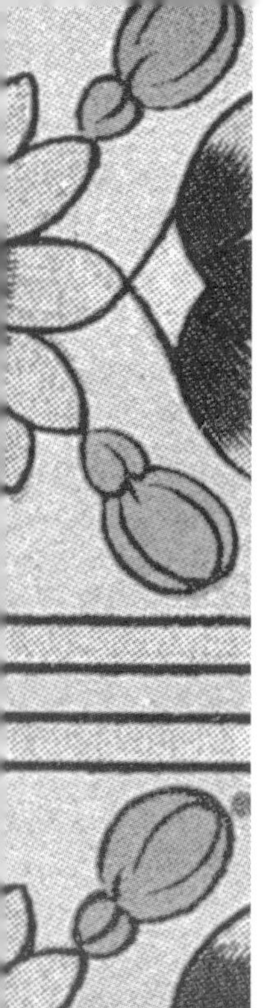

Don't design your stairs to lead toward a bathroom or the main entrance door of your home if you're remodeling.

Don't let your stove burners get dirty or encrusted with spillover food from your cooking. Clean burners facilitate wealth in your household.

Do face the E (wood element) or S (fire element) while standing at the burners of your kitchen stove.

Don't locate your stove under a window.

Do add more burners to your stove to increase your prosperity.

Don't choose a home with its stove on an island or peninsula, as an absence of a wall means absence of support for the family's finances.

Do tape or set a natural quartz crystal on the side of your telephone to activate more calls.

Do hang a hollow-rod wind chime above the telephone to encourage it to ring.

Do plan to have drainage water moving from right to left in front of your home if it faces NW, NE, SW, or SE.

Don't introduce the "other woman" into your home by activating more female yin energy in the form of a water feature on the right side (facing out the door) of your front yard.

Do add more water to the wood areas of E and SE. Wood represents spring and new beginnings, and is nurtured by the element of water.

Don't choose a home that has a drainage canal or ditch behind it, which is believed to transport your financial security away. Block the view with a wall, thick hedge, or row of trees.

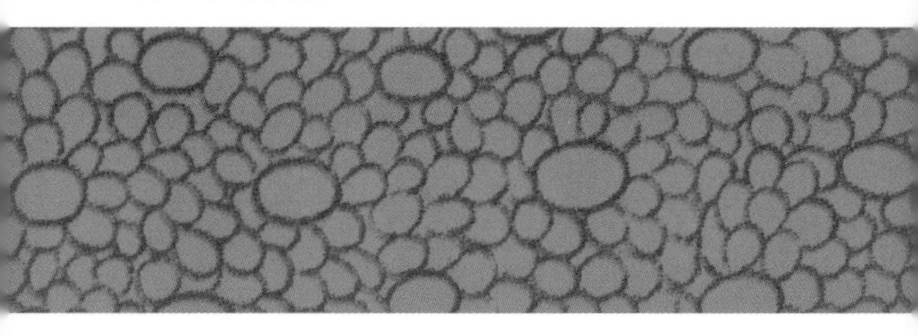

Do arrange to have water flowing from left to right in front of your entrance if your home faces a cardinal direction (such as N, S, E, or W), so wealth will be carried to your family.

Do keep a metal bowl of dried lotus seeds in the W area of your bedroom to encourage fertility.

Do add metal and metallic colors in the W to benefit your children and their creativity—but don't do so in the bedrooms, where this element is detrimental to your kids' health.

Do use the shapes of metal (circles, semicircles, arches, and so on) in the W.

Do put seven pairs of metal chopsticks in the W area of your dining room to increase your fertility.

Do let the strong yang energy of W's setting sun help uplift an elderly person or aid in the recovery of an ill person.

Do use pewter or silver vases to enhance the children area of the W.

Do activate the W (children) with earth and metal accessories.

"Pray not for gold. Pray for good children and happy grandchildren."

— Chinese proverb

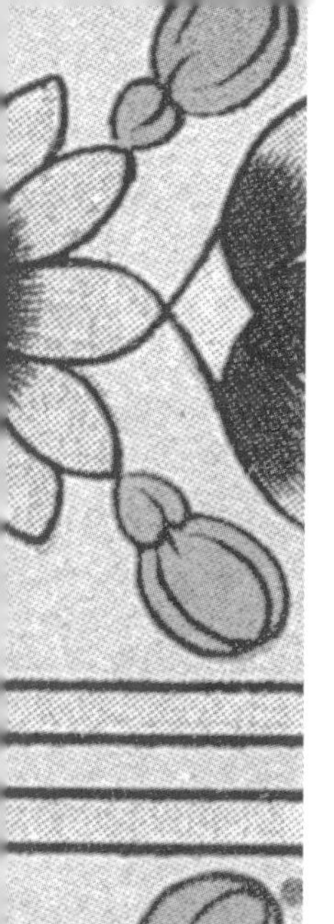

Do add the wood element into your kitchen in the form of chopping and butcher blocks, salad bowls, counters, stools, chairs, or a bowl of nuts.

Do surround yourself with more things made of wood if you have liver problems, as the liver is the yin component of wood.

Do add more wood in your home if you're feeling depressed, timid, or shy.

Don't keep wood articles, accessories, and furniture in your environment if you're feeling frustrated.

Do place more wood accessories and furniture in your home if you have a tendency to easily cry, if your fingernails are weak, or if your eyes itch.

Do group wooden furniture in fours in the SW area of your living room, for wood is the element of prosperity and abundance.

Do use a wooden box to store your bread, allowing it to breathe.

Figure G – The Chinese Zodiac.

Do use the set or group of the 12 animals of the Chinese zodiac for decoration and protection. It can be in the form of jewelry, carvings, wall hangings, or other art.

ABOUT THE AUTHOR

Angi Ma Wong is an internationally recognized feng shui expert/consultant and the best-selling author of the *Feng Shui Dos & Taboos* series. She has appeared on *The Oprah Winfrey Show, LIVE! with Regis and Kelly,* CNN, *CBS News Sunday Morning,* the Discovery Channel, and in *Time* magazine. Website: **www.FengShuiLady.com**.

NOTES

NOTES

NOTES

NOTES

NOTES

NOTES

NOTES

NOTES

We hope you enjoyed this Hay House Lifestyles book. If you would like to receive a free catalog featuring additional Hay House books and products, or if you would like information about the Hay Foundation, please contact:

Hay House, Inc.
P.O. Box 5100
Carlsbad, CA 92018-5100

(760) 431-7695 or **(800) 654-5126**
(760) 431-6948 (fax) or **(800) 650-5115 (fax)**
www.hayhouse.com® • www.hayfoundation.org

Published and distributed in Australia by: Hay House Australia Pty. Ltd., 18/36 Ralph St., Alexandria NSW 2015 • *Phone:* 612-9669-4299 • *Fax:* 612-9669-4144 • www.hayhouse.com.au

Published and distributed in the United Kingdom by: Hay House UK, Ltd., 292B Kensal Rd., London W10 5BE • *Phone:* 44-20-8962-1230 • *Fax:* 44-20-8962-1239 • www.hayhouse.co.uk

Published and distributed in the Republic of South Africa by: Hay House SA (Pty), Ltd., P.O. Box 990, Witkoppen 2068 • *Phone/Fax:* 27-11-706-6612 • orders@psdprom.co.za

Published in India by: Hay House Publishers India, Muskaan Complex, Plot No. 3, B-2, Vasant Kunj, New Delhi 110 070 • *Phone:* 91-11-4176-1620 • *Fax:* 91-11-4176-1630 • www.hayhouseindia.co.in

Distributed in Canada by: Raincoast , 9050 Shaughnessy St., Vancouver, B.C. V6P 6E5 • *Phone:* (604) 323-7100 • *Fax:* (604) 323-2600 • www.raincoast.com